VERBS

in

ACTION

LINDA A. FERREIRA

INTERMEDIATE DRILLS

PRESENT SIMPLE
PRESENT CONTINUOUS
PAST SIMPLE
PAST CONTINUOUS
PRESENT PERFECT
PRESENT PERFECT CONTINUOUS
PAST PERFECT
PAST PERFECT CONTINUOUS
FUTURE
FUTURE CONTINUOUS
FUTURE PERFECT
FUTURE PERFECT CONTINUOUS
CONDITIONALS
WISHES/HOPES
MODALS
PASSIVES

NEWBURY HOUSE PUBLISHERS, Cambridge
A division of Harper & Row, Publishers, Inc.
New York, Philadelphia, San Francisco, Washington
London, Mexico City, São Paulo, Singapore, Sydney

Library of Congress Cataloging in Publication Data

Ferreira, Linda A
    Verbs in action.

    1. English language—Text-books for foreign students.
2. English language—Verb. I. Title.
PE1128.F45   428.2'4   77-10886
ISBN 0-88377-097-0

Cover and book design by Diana Esterly.

NEWBURY HOUSE PUBLISHERS
A division of Harper & Row, Publishers, Inc.

Language Science
Language Teaching
Language Learning

CAMBRIDGE, MASSACHUSETTS

Printed in the U.S.A.   First printing: February 1978
                                               10 9 8 7 6

Table of Contents

Introduction

In learning a language, including English, the student must be exposed to *how* the language works. This need not be an extensive explanation of rules and examples on the part of the teacher. The concept of the structure is already known to the student from his native language. What the student has to learn is *how to express the message* he wishes to convey in a form understood as "correct" to speakers of the target language.

By an *internal* process, the student learning English tranforms the concept from his native language into comparable patterns of English structure. He is in reality translating the *idea*, not the words. For the student to do this, the new structures in the target language should be presented sequentially; new structures must be based on previously learned patterns, or at least presented in a framework that identifies the meaning and use of the new structure.

Drills, through repetition of the structure, can be especially helpful in reinforcing the pattern and in practicing word order, so important in English. However, if such drills are to be helpful in actually learning the language, they should be meaningful and allow the student to manipulate the language within a guided framework. Also, by practicing the use of the structure in everyday situations, the student can increase his communicating and fluency skills. In this way, drills, when carefully written, are useful tools in the language-learning process.

The *objective* of this text is to present guided practice on the tenses, allowing the student to manipulate the language to a point where the concept of the structure is internalized as the "correct" expression in English.

How to use this book

The tenses are presented in the sequence appearing in most ESL/EFL texts. However, each drill can be used independently, depending on the ability of the students and the sequence of the particular program in use. This format also allows for use in review and remedial work. All drills are on the intermediate level, in that they reflect appropriate vocabulary and sentence length. Since the purpose of the drills is to reinforce the structure and *not* to introduce specialized vocabulary, the situations are simple and straightforward.

Also included in this text are drills on conditionals, wishes, hopes, modals, and passives. These are important structures that cause students difficulty. The patterns are introduced through situational drills which help identify their particular use.

Method

It should be noted that the names and places used in the text might be altered by the teacher to reflect local names and places. For example, the name of a local supermarket might be substituted for "supermarket." In cases where the question is directed to a male, the cue "dress" would be inappropriate and should be changed to "suit." The teacher should preview each drill, making the necessary changes. By adapting the drills to suit each class, the teacher can create a more realistic situation, adding to the effectiveness of the practice.

Effort should be made to use the drills as naturally as possible. By holding the book in one hand and walking around the classroom, the teacher is creating an informal setting. Correct stress and intonation, as well as facial expression and body movement, are also important in communicating the patterns.

Since the prompts have been controlled for length, the teacher should not allow the students to look at their books, at least for the initial presentation. The drills could be repeated with one student asking another, or forming practice groups. The drills, done orally in class, could be assigned for written homework. This is especially recommended for the *modals*, where fine distinctions in meaning are made by native speakers.

Types of drills

Each drill is identified by a short title, followed by notes on usage whenever appropriate. The teacher's role is marked with a T; S1, S2, S3, etc., refer to student 1, student 2, student 3, etc. The first example of each drill includes the correct student response in italics.

Prompt words appear in parentheses. These are to be given by the teacher. The lead sentence should not be repeated after the first few times. By then, the students should know the correct response pattern:

Example: T: Where's   (Paris)?
           S: *It's in France.*
                London   (prompts)
                New York
                etc.

The sentence is repeated each time by the teacher, substituting the prompts for the word(s) in parentheses:

Where's London?
Where's New York?
etc.

Many drills require the student to use *cue* words or phrases. In this case, the sentence(s) and the cue must be given each time:

Example: T: The train is due at 6:45. It's 6:42 now.   (arrive) ← cue
            S: *The train is arriving now.*

Other drills require the teacher to give the students one or two sentences which have to be manipulated to form one sentence of the required pattern:

Example: T: She became a teacher last year.
          S1: *She's been a teacher for a year.*
               She's been a teacher since 19_____ .

Time graphs

Suggested activities for introducing tenses on time graphs[1] are presented at the beginning of each unit. In addition, time graphs provide a useful format for review and remedial work, especially for making distinctions for English tenses that may not have counterparts in the native language.

Time graphs provide *visual* reinforcement of tense patterns. The concepts of past, present, and future are represented as:

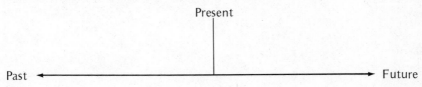

By marking points and lines on this graph to indicate the time relationships, the student forms the concept of the tense.

For example, the *past simple tense* is used for an event that occurred at a definite point in the past, represented as an x on the graph. On the other hand, the *past continuous tense* occurs over a period of time in the past, represented as a line drawn across the x:

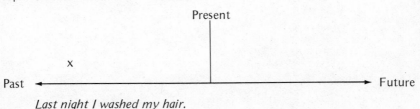

Last night I washed my hair.

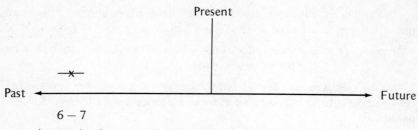

6 — 7

Last night, from 6 to 7 o'clock, I was washing my hair.

Tenses can also be contrasted, using the time graph:

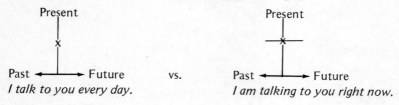

I talk to you every day.   vs.   *I am talking to you right now.*

1. First known use of time graph by Dorothy Danielson and Rebecca Hayden, *Mastering American English*, Prentice-Hall, Inc., Englewood Cliffs, New Jersey.

Present Simple Tense

To introduce the *present simple tense*

METHOD

      Draw a time graph on the blackboard.

      Say the following, marking each action with an x on the time graph.

T: Every day, I get up.

                   brush my teeth

                   comb my hair

                   eat breakfast

                   go to school

                   teach English

```
                          Present
                          x   get up
                          x   brush my teeth
                          x   comb my hair
                          x   eat breakfast
                          x   go to school
                          x   teach English
Past  ◄───────────────────┼──────────────────►  Future
```

REPEAT

Activity 1: Make a new time graph.

             Ask the students: "What do you do every day at school?"

             Mark on the time graph as above.

Activity 2: Make a new time graph.

             Ask the students: "What do you do on your vacation?"

             Mark on the time graph as above.

Used to express a fact

      The *present simple tense* is used to make statements that are permanently true, or at least true over a period of time, not just at the moment of speaking.

DRILL 1   To practice the *present simple tense* with *where*

A.   T: (the Eiffel Tower) Where is the Eiffel Tower?

          S1: *It's in Paris.*

T: (the Colosseum)
S2: *Where is the Colosseum?*
S3: *It's in Rome. It isn't in Paris.*

The Kremlin	Westminster Abbey
The Empire State Building	The Prado
Disneyland	The Topkapi Museum
The Parthenon	The World Trade Center
The Taj Mahal	The Loop
The Statue of Liberty	The Great Pyramids
The Louvre	

Note: *You may want to use local places and buildings more familiar to the students.*

B.   T: (the Nile River) Where is the Nile River?
      S1: *It's in Africa.*
      T: (the Amazon)
      S2: *Where is the Amazon River?*
      S3: *It's in South America. It isn't in Africa.*

The Mississippi River	The Ganges
The Seine	The Hudson
The Rhine	The Yukon
The Thames	The Rio Grande
The Yangtze	

C.   T: (Toronto) Where is Toronto?
      S1: *It's in Canada.*
      T: (London)
      S2: *Where is London?*
      S3: *It's in England. It isn't in Canada.*

Nairobi	Peking
Chicago	Rome
Lyon	Frankfurt
Liverpool	Amsterdam
Dublin	Damascus
Rio de Janeiro	Caracas
Moscow	Johannesberg

D.   T: (name of the local supermarket) Where is (name of the local supermarket)?
      S1: *It's on _____ Street.*
      T: (local theater)
      S2: *Where is (local theater)?*
      S3: *It's on _____ Street. It isn't on _____ Street.*

local cinema	local cafe
local department store	local government building
local restaurant	local clothing store
local museum	local zoo
local hotel	local post office
local university	local monument
local nightclub	local grocery store
local sports stadium	local jewelry store

DRILL 2   To practice the *present simple tense* with *when*

A.   T: When is Christmas?
   S1:   *Christmas is on December 25th.*
   T: (September 1st)
   S2:   *Is Christmas on September 1st?*
   S3:   *No, it isn't. Christmas is on December 25th.*

Thanksgiving	Easter
Independence Day	The first day of spring
Labor Day	The first day of winter
Valentine's Day	George Washington's birthday
Halloween	Memorial Day

B.   T: When is (local holiday)?

Note: *Have the students ask each other questions about dates of local holidays.*

DRILL 3   To practice the *present simple tense* with other *question words*

A.   *Present simple tense* with *how much*

   T: (A loaf of bread) costs 59 cents in New York City. How much does a loaf of bread cost in your city?
   S1:   *A loaf of bread costs _____ cents in _____ .*

S1 to
   S2:   *How much does a loaf of bread cost in your city?*
      etc.

Students ask each other the questions until all students have answered.

a quart of milk	a bottle of wine
a pound of tomatoes	an ice-cream cone
a dozen eggs	a pound of coffee
a pound of butter	a pound of cheese
a cup of coffee	a small chicken

B. *Present simple tense* with *how far*

T: How far is (Paris) from here?
S1: *Paris is _____ miles from here.*
T: (London)
S2: *How far is London from here?*
S3: *London is _____ miles from here.*

Chicago	Lisbon
Tokyo	Brasilia
San Francisco	Lagos
Rome	Beirut
Athens	Istanbul
Nairobi	Sydney
Boston	

local university	local post office
local museum	local monument
local recreation area	local zoo
local shopping area	local government building
local theater	local cinema

Note: *You may want to bring some world or city maps to class and have the students ask each other questions using the maps for reference.*

C. *Present simple tense* with *how many*

T: How many (inches are in a foot)?
S1: *There are 12 inches in a foot.*
T: Are there 10 inches in a foot?
S2: *No, there aren't. There are 12 inches in a foot.*
T: (feet in a yard)
S3: *How many feet are in a yard?*
S4: *There are 3 feet in a yard.*
T: Are there 4 feet in a yard?
S5: *No, there aren't. There are 3 feet in a yard.*
T: (ounces in a pound), etc.

pounds in a kilo	minutes in an hour
miles in a kilometer	hours in a day
inches in a meter	days in a week
seconds in a minute	days in a year

Note: *You may want to bring some metric and British rulers and scales into class, especially if the students are used to working in the metric system. Have the students ask each other questions, using the rulers as a guide.*
Sample questions: How wide is our English book? How long is our

English book? How tall is John? How wide is the room? How high is the desk? How deep is the wastepaper basket? etc.

D. *Present simple tense* with *what*

  T: What (tells the time)?
  S1: *A clock does.*
  T: (keeps food cold)
 S1 to
  S2: *What keeps food cold?*
  S2: *A refrigerator does.*
  T: (makes coffee), etc.

gives the months and the days	prints the news
plays records	toasts bread
takes pictures	makes ice
opens cans	pushes a nail into wood
records voices	dries hair
cuts the grass	washes clothes
cooks food	presses clothes
writes in ink	

Note: *To practice the negative* doesn't, *ask the students questions like:*

T: Does a toaster bake bread?
S: No, it doesn't. An oven does.

E. *Present simple tense* with *who*

  T: Who (delivers the mail)?
  S1: *A mailman does.*
  T: (sells flowers)
 S1 to
  S2: *Who sells flowers?*
  S2: *A florist does.*
  T: (sells meat), etc.

makes furniture	prescribes medicine
teaches school	makes suits
directs traffic	plays the piano
catches fish	writes books
fixes cars	bakes bread
repairs broken pipes	takes photographs
delivers milk	paints pictures
plays the violin	fixes teeth
flies a plane	cuts hair

Note: *To practice the negative* doesn't, *ask the students questions like:*

T: Does a mailman deliver milk?
S: No, he doesn't. A milkman delivers milk.

F.   *Present simple tense* with other *question words*

> T: What food do people in (your country) eat?
> S1:   *People in* (his country) *eat* _____ .
> S1 to
> S2:   *What food do people in* (your country) *eat?*
> S2:   *People in* (his country) *eat* _____ .
> S2 to
> S3:   *What food do people in* (your country) *eat?*

Students ask each other questions until all the students have answered.

What do people in (your country) drink?
What clothes do people in (your country) wear?
What kind of cars do people in (your country) drive?
What kind of cigarettes do people in (your country) smoke?
What kind of pets do people in (your country) have?
What kind of music do people in (your country) listen to?
What kind of movies do people in (your country) see?
What kinds of sports do people in (your country) play?
What time do the stores open in (your country)?
What time do the stores close in (your country)?
What time do the people in (your country) eat lunch?
What time do the people in (your country) eat dinner?

Used to express habits or repeated actions

The *present simple tense* is used to make statements about what is generally true, or at least true over a period of time. Note that the present tense is used for present *conditions* which may not be actually taking place at the moment of speaking. For example, a person may say "I take the bus to work," while *at the moment of speaking* he is talking to a friend in his office. This is a distinction in English that is not necessarily made in other languages.

DRILL 4   To practice the *present simple tense* with *habits*

A.   Habits taking place in the morning or in the evening

> T: Answer "in the morning" or "in the evening." When do you (do your homework)?
> S1:   *I do my homework in the evening.*
> S1 to
> S2:   *When do you do your homework?*
> S2:   *I do my homework in the morning.*
> T: (eat breakfast)
> S3:   *I eat breakfast in the morning.*

S3 to
  S4: *When do you eat breakfast?* etc.

watch television	brush your teeth
read a book	wash your clothes
have dinner	go to a discotheque
go to school	listen to records
wash your hair	read the newspaper
go to the movies	go to the bank
get your mail	listen to the radio
make your bed	

B. Habits taking place in the fall, in the winter, in the spring, or in the summer

  T: Answer "in the fall," "in the winter," "in the spring," or "in the summer." When do you (go skiing)?
  S1: *I go skiing in the winter.*
  T: When does (S1's name) go skiing?
  S2: *S1 goes skiing in the winter.*

play tennis	pick apples
wear a heavy coat	water ski
start school	turn on the heat
use the air conditioner	play football
wear shorts	wear a fur hat
go ice skating	build a snowman
drink ice tea	get a suntan
start your garden	wear sandals
drink hot chocolate	

C. Habits that are specific to each student

  T: Where do you (buy your shoes)?
  S1: *I buy my shoes at _____ .*
  S1 to
  S2: *Where do you buy your shoes?*
  S2: *I buy my shoes at _____ .*

Students ask each other the question until all students have answered.

buy magazines	eat Chinese food
study	get a pizza
read the newspaper	mail your letters
go dancing	keep your socks
get an ice-cream cone	pick up your mail
put your old letters	keep your money
go on Saturday night	buy your bread
do your laundry	meet your friends

D. Habits with *how many* and *how much*

      T: How many letters do you write (in) a month?

      S1: *I write 10 letters a month.*

   S1 to

      S2: *How many letters do you write a month?*

      S2: *I write 12 letters a month.*

Students ask each other the question until all students have answered.

Note: *To practice the third person singular, the teacher may ask: "How many letters does (S1's name) write a month?"*

    How many newspapers do you read every day?

    How much sugar do you take in your coffee?

    How many magazines do you read every week?

    How many hours of television do you watch every day?

    How much milk do you drink every day?

    How many hours do you sleep every day?

    How many telephone calls do you make every day?

    How many cigarettes do you smoke every day?

    How many times do you brush your teeth every day?

    How many times do you see your girlfriend (boyfriend) every day?

    How many times do you comb your hair every day?

    How many times do you shine your shoes every week?

    How many times do you wash your hair every month?

    How many times do you eat every day?

    How many records do you buy every year?

    How many times do you get angry every day?

DRILL 5   To practice the *present simple tense* with *frequency words*

Adverbs of frequency occur with the *present simple tense* when the speaker refers to his present habits and preferences. Put the following chart of frequency words on the blackboard and compare the meanings of the various frequency words:

Time occurring	Frequency words
100%	Always
90%	Usually
70%	Frequently, often
30%	Occasionally, sometimes
10%	Seldom, rarely, hardly ever, almost never
0%	Never

A. To practice *position* of frequency words in statements with action verbs in the *present simple tense*

T: How often do you do your homework?
S1: *I (always, often, etc.) do my homework.*

How often do you read the newspaper?
How often do you wash your own clothes?
How often do you answer your letters?
How often do you walk to school?
How often do you cook your own meals?
How often do you watch TV?
How often do you come to class on time?
How often do you make your own bed?
How often do you study for tests?
How often do you wash the dishes?
How often do you study for tests?
How often do you go out on Saturday nights?
How often do you return your library books on time?
How often do you go on diets?
How often do you think in English?
How often do you study at home?

B.   To practice the position of frequency words in statements with the verb
to be in the *present simple tense*

T: How often is the bus to school on time?
S: *The bus to school is (always, usually, etc.) on time.*

How often is this class interesting?
How often is this classroom clean?
How often is the homework difficult?
How often are the tests fair?
How often are the lessons hard?
How often is the food at school good?
How often are the tests difficult?
How often is the teacher fair?
How often is the book interesting?
How often is the class fun?

C.   To contrast the position of the frequency words *always* and *never* in
statements with *present simple verbs*

T: John comes to class after the bell every day.
S1: *John always comes to class after the bell.*
T: (late)
S2: *John is always late.*

John sees the doctor every day.   (sick)
John falls asleep in class every day.   (awake)
John sleeps late every day.   (tired)

John takes a shower every day. (dirty)
John falls asleep at every lecture. (bored)
John doesn't say a word in class. (quiet)
John makes friends with everyone he meets. (shy)
John doesn't make any mistakes. (careful)
John doesn't stop eating. (hungry)

D. To practice the meaning of the frequency words in statements in the *present simple tense*

Substitute the appropriate frequency word for the adverbs of frequency implied or used in these sentences:

T: John goes to the movies some of the time.
S: *He sometimes goes to the movies.*

John doesn't answer the telephone.
John visits his aunt once in a while.
John is bored in all his classes.
John works late almost every night.
John doesn't clean his room.
John goes to the theater some of the time.
John visits the dentist once in a while.
John goes to Florida almost every Christmas vacation.
John is tired some of the time.
John goes dancing once a year.
John brushes his teeth after breakfast and dinner.
John smiles at everybody.
John eats out almost every night.
John does his homework once in a while.
John is quiet in almost every class.

Used to express opinions

DRILL 6 To practice verbs of *sense* and *mental* perception that refer to an action at the moment of speaking but of which we have no control.

Note: *We choose to "listen to" something; we "hear" something "involuntarily." Verbs of perception, e.g.,* want, understand, believe, *have no beginning or end because they refer to a mental perception that simply exists or does not exist in the mind of the speaker. However, "think" and "feel" have* present continuous forms *when they express a mental process* in progress. *For example, "I'm thinking of taking a trip" or "I'm feeling fine today."*

A. To practice verbs seldom used in the continuous tense

T: Do you understand the rule?
S1: *No, I don't understand it, but S2 does.*
S2: *Yes, I understand the rule, but S3 doesn't.*

Do you smell the gas?	Do you enjoy football games?
Do you feel hot?	Do you think about food a lot?
Do you remember the number?	Do you recall his name?
Do you hear the car?	Do you see his point?
Do you believe the story?	Do you recognize that woman?
Do you agree with her?	Do you realize the danger?
Do you trust that man?	Do you want some more coffee?
Do you doubt his excuse?	Do you understand the lesson?
Do you know his name?	

B. To contrast the *present continuous tense* with verbs seldom used in the continuous forms

T: The cake is baking in the oven.   (smell gas)
S: *Do you smell gas?*

Mary is lending that man some money.   (trust him)
The teacher is explaining the rule.   (understand it)
John is talking to a girl.   (recognize her)
He is watching a movie.   (enjoy films)
Jack is looking up Betty's telephone number.   (remember it)
Susan is serving coffee.   (want a cup)
Judy is practicing a new song.   (hear her)
Bob is turning off the air conditioner.   (feel cold)
Michael is putting the math problem on the blackboard.   (think it's correct)
Bob is talking to the new teacher.   (know her name)
The girl is telling the policeman her story.   (believe her)
The fighting is increasing in the Middle East.   (realize the danger)
Joan is arguing with her husband.   (see his point)
Jack is complaining about the food.   (agree with him)
The teacher is listening to John's excuse.   (doubt his story)
John is talking to the new student.   (recall his name)

C. To use the *present tense* to express *preferences*

T: Do you like to smoke?
S1: *Yes, I do, but John doesn't like to smoke.*
S2: *No, I don't like to smoke, but John does.*
T: (hate to dance)
S2 to
S3: *Do you hate to dance?*

s, I do, but John doesn't hate to dance.
, I don't hate to dance, but John does.
elieve in life after death), etc.

efer small cars to big cars?
enjoy plane rides?
dislike French movies?
believe in Women's Liberation?
like to dress up?
enjoy the theater?
prefer classical music to jazz?
like Italian actresses?
hate the ballet?
prefer blonds to redheads?
hate to study?
enjoy speaking English?
believe in astrology?
like sports?
dislike hot foods?
hate formal dinners?
believe in flying saucers?
dislike modern art?

D. To use the verb *to be* to express opinions in the *present simple tense*

T: Is it good to smoke? (Answer "yes" or "no" and give a reason for your opinion.)
S1: *Yes, it's good to smoke. It helps you relax.*
S2: *No, it isn't good to smoke. It's bad for your health.*

Is it important to study?
Is it good to eat a lot of bread?
Is it good to drink a lot of milk?
Is it important to take vitamins?
Is it important to vote?
Is it bad to drink a lot of beer?
Is it important to earn a lot of money?
Is it bad to swim in the winter?
Is it important to go to the dentist twice a year?
Is it good to get married?
Is it bad to watch a lot of television?
Is it important to save money?
Is it good to marry young?
Is it important to have children?
Is it bad to eat meat?

Present Continuous Tense

To introduce the *present continuous tense*

METHOD

> Draw a time graph on the blackboard.
> Say the following, marking each action with an x, then drawing a line
> *across* the x to show continuing actions.

T: Every day, I teach English. Right now, I am teaching English.
> write on the blackboard. Right now, I am writing on the
> blackboard.
> teach a lesson. Right now, I am teaching a lesson.
> stand in front of the class. Right now, I am standing in
> front of the class.

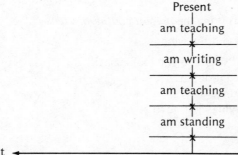

```
                        Present
                          |
                    am teaching
                _____x_____
                    am writing
                _____x_____
                    am teaching
                _____x_____
                    am standing
                _____x_____
                          |
Past ◄────────────────────┼────────────────────► Future
```

REPEAT

Activity 1: Make a new time graph.
> Ask the students: "What do you do in class every day? What are
> you doing right now?"
> Mark on the time graph as above.

Activity 2: Make a new time graph.
> Ask the students: "What does the milkman do every day?
> > mailman
> > florist
> > butcher
> > policeman
> > etc.
>
> What is he doing right now?"
> Mark on the time graph as above.

Used to express actions occurring at the moment of speaking

DRILL 7   Actions to introduce the *present continuous tense*

A.   T: Walk across the room. *While* you are walking across the room, say: "I am walking across the room." Repeat the action, saying: "What am I doing right now?"

     S: *You are walking across the room.*

Repeat for the following actions:

open a book	close the window
close a book	sit down in a chair
pick up a pencil	stand up
write on the blackboard	put on your coat
open the door	take out some money
close the door	give a pen to a student
look out the window	comb your hair
open the window	

B.   Questions to ask students using the *present continuous tense*

Ask the students to look out the window.

T: Ask the students: "What are you looking at?"
T: What are you thinking about?
T: What are you wearing?
T: What are you studying right now?

DRILL 8   Actions to review the *present continuous tense*

A.   Act out each group of actions. Just before each *group* is completed, ask the students "What am I doing?" Repeat the *group* of actions. During each individual action, ask "What am I doing?" *if the students know the appropriate vocabulary.* Have the students act out the actions for the class.

1.   Getting dressed (actions to be performed by the teacher)

yawn and stretch	put on the clothes
rub your eyes	put on socks/shoes
walk to the closet and open the door	put on watch/earrings
take out a dress/suit	

2.   Lighting a cigarette (actions to be performed by the teacher)
take out a cigarette packet from your purse/pocket
knock out a cigarette
put the cigarette in your mouth

strike a match
light the cigarette
take a puff
knock off the ash in the ashtray
take a puff
put the cigarette out

3. Making a bed (actions to be performed by the teacher)
get out of bed
gather up the bedding
throw the bedding to one side
open up a fresh sheet
throw the sheet on the bed
tuck in the corners
throw on the top sheet
throw on the blankets
tuck in the corners
turn down the top sheet and blanket
put the pillows in the pillowcases
fluff up the pillows and throw them on the bed
throw on the spread and arrange the pillows

4. Opening a bottle of wine (actions to be performed by the teacher)
wipe off the bottle   pull out the cork
put in the corkscrew   pour the first glass
twist the corkscrew   take a sip

5. Making fried eggs (actions to be performed by the teacher)
grease the frying pan
break the eggs on the rim of the pan
shake the pan
flip the eggs
slide the eggs onto the plate

B. Acting out individual actions to review the *present continuous tense*

T: Act out the following actions or write the action on a piece of paper and give to a student to act out. (You could whisper the action to the student to save time.) Let the student act out the action while the rest of the students guess what he is doing.

S1:   (taking a photograph) While he is acting out taking a photograph, he says *What am I doing?*

S2:   *Are you taking a photograph?*

S1:   *Yes, I'm taking a photograph.*

Actions to be performed by the students.

knitting	serving a tennis ball
changing a flat tire	setting an alarm clock
ice skating	tying a shoelace
driving a car	reading a book
shaving	changing a baby's diaper
washing my hair	playing basketball
playing a record	shining shoes
typing	making a phone call
threading a needle and sewing	swimming
directing traffic	watching TV
making a dive	opening a can
skiing	playing football

Note: *You can make this into a game by dividing the students into two teams and setting a time limit in which to guess. The team with more successful guesses wins.*

DRILL 9   To practice the *present continuous tense* with *unseen* actions occurring *continuously* in the present

T: What's happening in the city right now?
    What's the mailman doing right now?   (deliver mail)
    The mailman is delivering mail right now.
    (the milkman)
S1: *What's the milkman doing right now?*
T: (deliver milk)
S2: *The milkman is delivering milk right now.*

The policeman   (direct traffic)
The taxi driver   (pick up people)
The plumber   (fix pipes)
The dentist   (pull teeth)
The baker   (bake bread)
The mechanic   (fix cars)
The tailor   (make suits)
The grocer   (sell vegetables)
The butcher   (cut meat)
The hairdresser   (wash hair)
The truck driver   (drive a truck)
The pilot   (fly a plane)
The nurse   (take care of sick people)
The florist   (sell flowers)
The fireman   (put out fires)

DRILL 10   To contrast the *present simple tense* with the *present continuous tense*

A.   T: Draw a clock on the blackboard. Indicate the time span (e.g., from 2 to 8 p.m.) by moving your finger from 2 to 8 and then back again. Then point to the exact time (e.g., 4 o'clock). John drives a taxi from 2 to 8 p.m. every day. (indicate the time span) It's 4 o'clock now. (point to 4 o'clock) What is John doing right now?

   S1:   *John's driving a taxi right now.*

   T: What does John do every day from 2 to 8 p.m.?

   S2:   *John drives a taxi from 2 to 8 p.m. every day.*

Repeat for:

Mȧry teaches school from 9 to 3 every day. It's 11 o'clock now.
Steven studies from 7 to 10 every day. It's 8 o'clock now.
Michael writes letters from 8 to 9 every Sunday. It's 7 o'clock now.
Susan models clothes from 7 to 12 every morning. It's 10 o'clock now.
Bob delivers mail from 8 to 4 every day. It's 2 o'clock now.
Mr. Williams eats lunch from 12 to 1 every day. It's 12:30 now.
Barbara watches the news from 5 to 7:30 every week day. It's 6 o'clock now.
Richard plays tennis from 4 to 6 every afternoon. It's 3 o'clock now.
George listens to music every night after dinner. It's 9 o'clock now.
Judy washes the dishes every night. It's after dinner now.
Jim brushes his teeth after every meal. It's after breakfast now.
Bob takes a nap after lunch every day. It's after lunch now.
Jane washes her hair every Sunday night. It's Sunday right now.

B.   Ask the students to tell you what their father (brother, mother, sister, etc.) does every day. For example:

   S1:   *My father works on his farm every day.*

   S2 to

   S1:   *What is your father doing right now?*

   S1:   *My father is planting corn right now.*

C.   T: The plane is due at 12:30. It's 12:29 now.   (land)

   S: *The plane is landing now.*

The train is due at 6:45. It's 6:44 now.   (arrive)
The ship is due at 9:55. It's 9:50 now.   (dock)
The truck is due at 2:30. It's 2:29 now.   (pull in)
The guests are due at 7:30. It's 7:25 now.   (arrive)
The plane is due at 5:00. It's 4:50 now.   (land)
The food is due at 8:00. It's 7:55 now.   (come)
The bus is due at 11:30. It's 11:28 now.   (pull in)

The mail is due at 10:30. It's 10:29 now.   (come)
The students are due at 9:30. It's 9:25 now.   (arrive)

Used to express an action continuing over a period of time

DRILL 11   To contrast the *present simple tense* with the *present continuous tense* with actions continuing over a period of time

T: Where is Nixon now?   (live/California)
S: *He's living in California now.*

Robert Redford   (make a movie/Spain)
Kissinger   (travel/Middle East)
Jackie Onassis   (visit/Paris)
John Lennon   (sing/Liverpool)
Mohammed Ali   (fight/Zaire)
Billie Jean King   (play tennis/Wimbledon)
Solzhenitsyn   (write/Vermont)
Ingmar Bergman   (film/Sweden)
Brigitte Bardot   (swim/Riviera)
The Rolling Stones   (sing/San Francisco)
Nureyev   (dance/Canada)
Sophia Loren   (film/Rome)
Pele   (play soccer/New York)
Jacques Cousteau   (sail/Indian Ocean)

Note: *Ask the students to make up questions to ask each other about famous people in the news.*

DRILL 12   To contrast the *past tense* with the *present continuous tense* with actions continuing over a period of time

T: Last year I studied French. This year . . .   (English)
S: *This year I'm studying English.*

Last year, John lived in Paris. This year . . .   (New York)
Last year, Mary wrote short stores. This year . . .   (novel)
Last year, Jack traveled in Africa. This year . . .   (Japan)
Last year, Barbara studied at the Sorbonne. This year . . .
   (Harvard)
Last year, the Browns lived in a rented apartment. This year . . .
   (house)
Last year, Bob drove a Volkswagen. This year . . .   (Ford)
Last year, the Wilsons bought a house. This year . . .   (car)

Last year, Betty had a baby. This year . . .   (twins)
Last year, Mr. Smith grew roses. This year . . .   (daisies)
Last year, Carl studied history. This year . . .   (science)
Last year, Jackie visited her uncle. This year . . .   (cousins)
Last year, Mr. and Mrs. Hill raised dogs. This year . . .   (horses)
Last year, John read *Newsweek*. This year . . .   (*Time*)
Last year, Mary took the bus. This year . . .   (train)
Last year, Jane flew to Rome. This year . . .   (Paris)

Used to express future actions

DRILL 13   To practice the *present continuous tense* with future events

A.   T: Are you free tonight?   (visit a friend)
        S1:   *No, I'm visiting a friend.*
    S1 to
        S2:   *Are you free tonight?*
        T: (play tennis)
        S2:   *No, I'm playing tennis.*
    S2 to
        S3:   *Are you free tonight?*
        T: (see a film), etc.

go to a play	go to a football game
play chess	listen to my new records
eat out with a friend	clean the house
do homework	write letters
watch TV	go to bed early
wash my hair	study for a test
see my boyfriend	

B.   Questions to ask the students

        T: What are you doing this weekend?
        S1:   *I'm visiting a friend this weekend.*
    S1 to
        S2:   *What are you doing this weekend?*, etc.

What are you doing tonight?
What are you getting for Christmas? (your birthday)
Where are you going this summer?
What are you buying at the store?
Who(m) are you visiting next week?
What are you cooking for dinner?
When are you seeing the film?

When are you going to the dentist?
When are you doing your homework?
What are you watching on TV tonight?

C.   T: What are you doing on your trip to New York?   (Statue of
           Liberty)
      S: *We're visiting the Statue of Liberty.*

Paris   (The Eiffel Tower)
Rome   (The Colosseum)
Berlin   (The Berlin Wall)
London   (Big Ben)
China   (The Great Wall)
Zambia   (Victoria Falls)
Egypt   (The Great Pyramids)
Ireland   (The Blarney Stone)
California (Disneyland)
Peru   (Machu Picchu)
Moscow   (The Kremlin)
Athens   (The Acropolis)
India   (The Taj Mahal)
Madrid   (The Prado)
Morocco   (The Casbah)
Istanbul   (The Topkapi Museum)
Israel   (The Wailing Wall)

DRILL 14   To contrast the *present continuous tense* with an action *at the
moment of speaking* and the *present continuous tense* with a *future* action

T: Why are you wearing tennis shoes?   (play)
S: *I'm playing tennis later.*

Why are you wearing a bathing suit?   (swim)
Why are you carrying skis?   (ski)
Why are you wearing riding boots?   (ride)
Why are you carrying a football?   (play)
Why are you wearing an apron?   (bake)
Why are you carrying your luggage?   (leave for a trip)
Why are you carrying ice skates?   (skate)
Why are you wearing a golf cap?   (golf)
Why are you carrying a tennis racket?   (play)
Why are you wearing garden gloves?   (dig)
Why are you carrying your books?   (study)

Why are you carrying your tools?   (build a bookcase)
Why are you carrying a basketball?   (play)
Why are you wearing a sweatsuit?   (jog)
Why are you wearing a lot of makeup?   (see my boyfriend)
Why are you carrying a camera?   (take some photographs)

Past Simple Tense

To introduce the *past simple tense*

METHOD

     Draw a time graph on the blackboard.
     Say the following, marking each past action with an x on the time
       graph.

T: This morning, I got up at 7 o'clock.
                brushed my teeth
                took a shower
                put on my clothes
                ate breakfast
                went to school

```
                                    Present
   x got up                            |
     x brushed my teeth                |
       x took a shower                 |
         x put on my clothes           |
           x ate breakfast             |
             x went to school          |
                                       |
Past <---------------------------------+-------------------> Future
```

REPEAT

Activity 1: Make a new time graph.
             Ask the students: "What did you do this morning?"
             Mark on the time graph as above.

Activity 2: Make a new time graph.
             Ask the students: "What did you do last night?"
             Mark on the time graph as above.

Activity 3: Make a new time graph.
             Ask the students: "What did you do (last year, yesterday, etc.)?"
             Mark on the time graph as above.

**Used to make statements about facts or completed actions that
occurred at *one point* in the past**

DRILL 15   Actions to introduce the *past simple tense* of regular verbs

T: Walk across the room. After each action *is completed*, say "I walked across the room." (You might turn and look or point to the spot where the action took place.)

Repeat the action. *Then,* ask the students: "What did I do?"

S1:   *You walked across the room.*

Repeat for the following actions

(actions to practice -t, -d, and -id endings of past forms; be sure to check the students' pronunciation of the endings).

-t endings of past forms:
   look out the window
   knock on the window
   ask a question
   pick up a pencil

-d endings of past forms:
   open the window
   close the window
   pull up your socks
   comb your hair

-id endings of past forms:
   count your papers
   point at a student
   collect the homework
   fold a piece of paper

DRILL 16   To practice the pronunciation of the past endings of regular verbs

A.   To practice -t endings of regular verbs in the *past simple tense*

   T: Did you ask the question?
   S1:   *Yes, I asked the question.*
S1 to
   S2:   *Did you ask the question?*
   S2:   *No, I didn't. You asked the question.*

Repeat for:

Did you look on the table?   Did you help your mother?
Did you pick up your clothes?   Did you laugh at the joke?
Did you drop the dish?   Did you dance at the party?
Did you finish the test?   Did you wash the clothes?

Did you practice the song?   Did you smoke the last cigarette?
Did you knock on the door?   Did you talk to the man?
Did you cook the food?   Did you ask his name?
Did you walk to school?

B.   To practice -d endings of regular verbs in the *past simple tense*

     T: Did you pull the curtains?
     S1:   *Yes, I pulled the curtains.*
  S1 to
     S2:   *Did you pull the curtains?*
     S2:   *No, I didn't. You pulled the curtains.*

Repeat for:

Did you play with the children?   Did you use the car?
Did you learn the lesson?   Did you explain it to her?
Did you travel with John?   Did you arrive on time?
Did you open the mail?   Did you comb your hair?
Did you close the window?   Did you carry her books?
Did you happen to see the accident?   Did you study for the test?
Did you stay for the movie?   Did you marry that girl?
Did you borrow the money?

C.   To practice -id endings of regular verbs in the *past simple tense*

     T: Did you count the chairs?
     S1:   *Yes, I counted the chairs.*
  S1 to
     S2:   *Did you count the chairs?*
     S2:   *No, I didn't. You counted the chairs.*

Repeat for:

Did you fold the clothes?   Did you lift the box?
Did you collect the money?   Did you want to come?
Did you mount the horse?   Did you knit the sweater?
Did you load the truck?   Did you repeat the class?
Did you grate the cheese?   Did you expect to see her?
Did you braid the rug?   Did you wait for a long time?

D.   To practice -t, -d and -id endings of regular verbs in the *past simple tense*

     T: Did you lock the door or the window?
     S: *I locked the door.*
  or   *I locked the window.*

Did you learn English or French?
Did he count the chairs or the tables?
Did they pick up the food or the wine?

Did they finish the book or the magazine?
Did he borrow the car or the truck?
Did she ask for tea or coffee?
Did they collect the tickets or the money?
Did she close the door or the window? ·
Did he expect Mary or Betty?
Did they use the boat or the car?
Did she help her brother or her sister?
Did she knit the sweater or the hat?
Did you look for the money or the watch?
Did he drop the glass or the dish?
Did they walk to school or to the post office?
Did they wash the car or the truck?
Did she cook the chicken or the fish?
Did he load the car or the truck?
Did she play with the dog or the cat?
Did you practice the violin or the piano?
Did he smoke the cigar or the cigarette?

DRILL 17   To practice the *past simple* form of the verb *to be*

A.   To practice the third person singular of the *past simple* form of the verb *to be*

    T: Is John tired now?
    S1: *No, he isn't. But he was tired yesterday.*
    T: Was John tired last week?
    S2: *No, he wasn't tired last week.*
    T: (sick)
    S1: *Is John sick now?*
    S2: *No, he isn't. But he was sick yesterday.*
    T: (last week)
S2 to
    S3: *Was John sick last week?*
    S3: *No, he wasn't sick last week.*

Repeat for:

happy	depressed
upset	sad
bored	careful
quiet	exhausted
angry	afraid
worried	

B. To practice the third person plural of the *past simple* form of the verb *to be*

> T: Are they tired now?
> S1: *No, they aren't. But they were tired yesterday.*
> T: Were they tired last week?
> S2: *No, they weren't tired last week.*
> T: (sick)
> S1: *Are they sick now?*
> S2: *No, they aren't. But they were sick yesterday.*
> T: (last week)
>
> S2 to
> S3: *Were they sick last week?*
> S3: *No, they weren't sick last week.*

Repeat for:

happy	depressed
upset	sad
bored	careful
quiet	exhausted
angry	afraid
worried	

C. To review the *past simple* form of the verb *to be*

> T: My friend went to medical school in 1970.   (student)
> S: *He was a medical student in 1970.*

My sisters went to nursing school in 1974.   (students)
My cousin went into the Navy in 1971.   (sailor)
My brothers went to camp in 1973.   (campers)
My aunt went to secretarial school in 1975.   (student)
My friends worked in a bakery in 1968.   (bakers)
My teacher taught history in 1973.   (teacher)
My horses won 10 races in 1976.   (winners)
My brothers became boy scouts in 1974.   (scouts)
My friend gave a concert in 1972.   (pianist)
My father starred in a Broadway play in 1950.   (actor)
My mother worked for TWA in 1952.   (stewardess)
My grandfather fought in World War I.   (soldier)
My uncle ran in the 1972 Olympics.   (athlete)
My brothers worked in a circus in 1968.   (clowns)
My dog won the dog show in 1973.   (champion)
My uncle voted democratic in 1960.   (Democrat)
My brother studied karate in 1974.   (black-belt)

DRILL 18   To introduce the *past simple* form of irregular verbs

A.   Ask the students to tell you what they do *every morning.* List the
actions on the blackboard. For example:

get out of bed	brush my teeth
wash my face	eat breakfast
comb my hair	go to school

Pointing to each action, go through the list saying: "Every morning, I
get out of bed. *This morning, I got out of bed at 8 o'clock."* (Continue, until
the list is completed.)

Repeat the process, writing the past tense forms on the blackboard. You
might circle the irregular verbs, pointing out that the students just have to
learn, by memorizing and practicing, these "exceptions."

B.   Ask the students to tell you what they normally do *at a party.* List the
actions on the blackboard. For example:

dance a lot	meet new people
eat hors d'oeuvres	laugh at jokes
drink wine	listen to music
talk to friends	tell stories

Pointing to each action, go through the list saying: "At every party, I
dance a lot. *Last night, I went to a party, I danced a lot."* (Continue, until the
list is completed.)

Repeat the process, writing the past tense forms on the blackboard. You
might circle the irregular verbs, pointing out that the students just have to
learn, by memorizing and practicing, these "exceptions."

Repeat for:

> things you do every day at school
> things you do at Christmas
> things you do on a vacation
> things you do in a supermarket
> etc.

DRILL 19   To practice the *past simple* forms of irregular verbs

T: Did he give you a pen or a pencil?
S: *He gave me a pen.*
or   *He gave me a pencil.*

A.   Did she eat the cake or the cookies?
Did she give you a shirt or a hat?
Did he come early or late?
Did she become a doctor or a lawyer?

Did he lie down at 10 or 11 o'clock?
Did he lay the mail on the desk or on the table?
Did she make one or two cakes?

B.   Did the party begin early or late?
Did the boat sink in the Atlantic or the Pacific Ocean?
Did he swim alone or with his friend?
Did he run in the first or the second race?
Did he drink the milk or the coke?
Did the bell ring early or late?
Did he sing the first or the second song?
Did he have chicken or steak?
Did he sit on the chair or on the floor?

C.   Did she teach English or French?
Did she think it was a good movie or a bad movie?
Did she bring the dog or the cat?
Did she buy the red coat or the blue coat?
Did he catch a big fish or a little fish?
Did she fight with Jack or with Bob?

D.   Did the dog bite Susan or Mary?
Did you do the first or the second exercise?
Did you light the lamp or the candle?
Did you hide the money or the jewels?
Did you slide on the ice or on the snow?

E.   Did you break your arm or your leg?
Did you choose the big one or the little one?
Did you drive the car or the motorcycle?
Did you freeze the steak or the chicken?
Did you ride the horse or the pony?
Did you rise at 8 or 9 o'clock?
Did you sell the house or the car?
Did the sun shine this morning or this afternoon?
Did you speak to John or to Jerry?
Did he steal the TV or the stereo?
Did he swear to give up smoking or to give up drinking?
Did he tear his sweater or his shirt?
Did he tell Mary or Betty?
Did he wake his sister or his brother?
Did he wear the blue shirt or the green one?
Did she write the letter to Jack or to Bill?

F.   Did the wind blow from the north or from the south?
Did he draw the fruit or the flowers?

Did he fly to London or to Paris?
Did he know the first or the second question?
Did John throw the football or the basketball?

G.   Did she fall on her face or on her back?
Did you feed the dog or the cat?
Did they hold a party or a dance?
Did he keep one or two kittens?
Did Margaret or Betty lead the parade?
Did she leave the party early or late?
Did Bob or Frank lend you the money?
Did she mean to meet here or at my house?
Did you meet her at school or at work?
Did you read his first or his second book?
Did he bend the pipe to the right or to the left?
Did she send John a card or a letter?
Did she sleep until 9 or 10 o'clock?
Did she spend $10 or $20?
Did he go to the theater or to the movies?

H.   Did he get a good grade or a bad grade?
Did he shoot a man or a woman?
Did he forget his hat or his coat?

I.   Did you take the bus or a taxi?
Did you stand at the front door or the back door?
Did you understand the French or the Italian movie?
Did you shake the mop or the broom?

J.   Did you dig the big hole or the little hole?
Did you hang the mirror or the picture?
Did John or George stick the stamp on the letter?
Did he strike gold or silver?

K.   Did she beat the eggs or the cream?
Did it cost $50 or $100?
Did he cut his knee or his face?
Did Jack or Jim hit the ball?
Did she hurt her hand or her foot?
Did she let him borrow the pen or the pencil?
Did she put on the red dress or the blue dress?
Did Betty or Jim set the table?
Did he shut the door or the window?

L.   Did he see Mary or Jane?
Did he say "yes" or "no"?

Did he hear the doorbell or the telephone?
Did he find $10 or $20?
Did he win the first or the second race?
Did he lose his hat or his coat?
Did he build a small or a big house?

DRILL 20   To practice questions and short answers of verbs in the *past simple tense*

A.   To practice the *past simple tense* with "last summer"

    T: Did you swim a lot last summer?
    S1:   *Yes, I did. I swam every day last summer.*
  S1 to
    S2:   *Did you swim a lot last summer?*
    S2:   *No, I didn't.*
  S2 to
    S3:   *Did you swim a lot last summer?*, etc.

Did you climb mountains a lot last summer?
Did you water ski a lot last summer?
Did you sail a lot last summer?
Did you camp a lot last summer?
Did you hike a lot last summer?
Did you play tennis a lot last summer?
Did you travel a lot last summer?
Did you walk along the beach a lot last summer?
Did you play football a lot last summer?
Did you eat outdoors a lot last summer?

B.   To practice the *past simple tense* with "last semester"

    T: Did you study English last semester?
    S1:   *Yes, I did. I studied English every day last semester.*
  S1 to
    S2:   *Did you study English last semester?*
    S2:   *No, I didn't.*
  S2 to
    S3:   *Did you study English last semester?*, etc.

Did you do a lot of homework last semester?
Did you use the library last semester?
Did you eat in the cafeteria last semester?
Did you see the principal last semester?
Did you go to classes last semester?
Did you take tests last semester?

Did you lose your book last semester?
Did you use the language laboratory last semester?
Did you read a lot of books last semester?
Did you go on a field trip last semester?
Did you ride the school bus last semester?

C.   To practice the *past simple tense* with "last night"

    T: Did you go home early last night?
    S1: *Yes, I did. I went home early last night.*
  S1 to
    S2: *Did you go home early last night?*
    S2: *No, I didn't.*
  S2 to
    S3: *Did you go home early last night?*, etc.

Did you stop for a cup of coffee last night?
Did you buy a newspaper last night?
Did you listen to the radio last night?
Did you watch TV last night?
Did you see a movie last night?
Did you go to a play last night?
Did you telephone your friends last night?
Did you take the bus last night?
Did you take a bath last night?
Did you wash your hair last night?
Did you sleep well last night?
Did you go to bed late last night?
Did you set the alarm last night?
Did you kiss your mother goodnight last night?

DRILL 21   To practice *question words* with the *past simple tense*

A.   T: What did you eat for dinner last night?
    S1: *Last night I ate _____ for dinner.*
  S1 to
    S2: *What did you eat for dinner last night?*
    S2: *Last night I ate _____ for dinner.* etc.

Where did you go yesterday afternoon?
What languages did you study last year?
How far did you walk last evening?
Who(m) did you see on the way to school today?
How much did that coat cost?
How many times did you try to call me yesterday?

How long did you study last night?
How many movies did you see last month?
How much medicine did you take last night?
How much money did you spend last week?
How much beer did you have last night?
How did you get to the airport last week?
Who took you to the bus station yesterday?
How did you find out about it?
Who gave the party?
When did you call me last night?
How long did you watch TV last night?
How many records did you buy last year?
When did you get home last night?
Where did you study last night?
What test did you take last week?
Where did you travel to last summer?
When did you get here?
What time did you fall asleep last night?
What did you watch on TV last night?

B.   T: I worked in a store once.   (when)
  S1 to
    S2:   *When did you work in a store?*
    S2:   *I worked in a store in 19 _____ .*
  S2 to
    S3:   *What did you do?*
    S3:   *I sold _____ .*

I worked in a bakery once.   (when) (what/do)
I worked in a supermarket once.   (when) (what/do)
I worked in a gas station once.   (when) (what/do)
I worked in a factory once.   (when) (what/do)
I worked in a school once.   (when) (what/do)
I worked in a restaurant once.   (when) (what/do)
I worked in a department store once.   (when) (what/do)
I worked in a hospital once.   (when) (what/do)
I worked in a nightclub once.   (when) (what/do)
I worked in a zoo once.   (when) (what/do)
I worked in a circus once.   (when) (what/do)
I worked in a hotel once.   (when) (what/do)

Note: *Ask students to tell about their own work experiences. Then, the other students can ask questions, using* when, where, what, how long, how much money *(did you make), etc.*

DRILL 22   To practice *ago* with the *past simple tense*

A.   T: When did you (see that movie)?   (2 weeks)
     S: *I saw that movie two weeks ago.*

   write that letter   (2 nights)
   visit that museum   (a month)
   travel to Canada   (a long time)
   open the mail   (10 minutes)
   eat your lunch   (an hour)
   get your driver's license   (a few years)
   give a party   (3 weeks)
   read that book   . (6 months)
   take her out   (a few weeks)
   buy that car   (over a year)
   cut your hair   (less than a week)
   move to your new house   (weeks)
   get married   (years)
   have the operation   (months)

B.   T: When was the last time you (had a cigarette)?
     S: *The last time I had a cigarette was _____ ago.*

   ate a pizza   had caviar
   cut your hair   went to a football game
   had Chinese food   sent flowers to your girlfriend
   wrote your mother   wrote a poem
   saw your girlfriend   changed the oil in your car
   took a shower   watered your plants
   had champagne   saw a good movie
   took a taxi   talked to your boyfriend
   saw a play   won some money in the lottery
   went to a discotheque

DRILL 23   To practice *when* with an action completed at *the same moment in the past*

A.   T: When did you (see her)?   (arrive)
     S: *I saw her when she arrived.*

   stop the car   (light/change)
   drop the dish   (hear/the noise)
   see the dog   (jump on me)
   shut off the TV   (program/end)
   go to the door   (doorbell/ring)
   write her   (get her letter)

find the book   (look in the desk)
hurt your back   (pick up the box)
get sick   (eat the bad apple)
come   (get your message)
fall down   (step on the ice)
burn your finger   (touch the hot iron)

B.   T: As a child, I (ate too much).   (I got sick)
          S: *When I ate too much, I got sick.*

cried   (my mother came)
played with matches   (I got punished)
got dirty   (my mother washed me)
talked too much   (my mother told me to be quiet)
played school   (I was the teacher)
got sick   (my mother gave me medicine)
got tired   (I took a nap)
ate a lot of cookies   (I got a stomachache)
played football   (I was captain)
went to the park   (I played on the swings)

Note: *Ask the students to tell you things they did "when they were children" or you can ask them:*

What happened when you cried?
What happened when you got sick?
What happened when you did something wrong?
What happened when you got bad grades in school?
etc.

DRILL 24   To practice the *past simple tense* with *reported* speech

Note: *Although native speakers are sometimes lax in using the correct sequence of tense with reported speech, students should be familiar with the correct form. A good way to do this is to use the analogy of a telephone conversation that can be depicted on the blackboard, using stick figures. Draw Bob, who is talking to John on the telephone. Bob's friend Bill is standing next to him.*

John (on the telephone): I'm tired.
Bob tells Bill: John says he's tired.
Bill: Sorry, I didn't hear you. What did *John say?*
Bob: John said he was tired.

A.   To practice the *past simple tense* of the verb *to be* with reported speech

          T: Dinner is ready.
          S1:   John *says* dinner *is* ready.

S2:   What *did* John *say*?

(S3:) John *said* dinner *was* ready.

John said The plane is late.   The train is early.

The bus is early.   The children are in school.

He's 25 years old today.   The baby is ill.

The car is for sale.   The room is cold.

The dinner is expensive.   The window is dirty.

The phone is busy.   The flowers are beautiful.

The food is cold.   The children are tired.

The sky is cloudy.

B. To practice the *past simple tense* with *reported* speech

T: Do you want to stay? (I asked them . . .)

S: *I asked them if they wanted to stay.*

Are they still tired? I wanted to know . . .

Does she want the book? I wasn't sure . . .

Do you like French movies? I wondered . . .

Is he sick? Did you notice . . .

Does he speak English? I wanted to know . . .

Are they ready? I wasn't sure . . .

Does she take tennis lessons? I wondered . . .

Do you take sugar or cream? I asked her . . .

Is she shy? Did you remember . . .

Does he drive? I wasn't sure . . .

Are they late? I wondered . . .

Does he smoke? I couldn't recall . . .

Is she tired? Did you notice . . .

Does he play football? I wondered . . .

Is she bored? I asked her . . .

Do they study a lot? I wanted to know . . .

Does he want a ride home? I wasn't sure . . .

Does he understand Spanish? I couldn't recall . . .

C. To practice the *past simple tense* and question words with *reported* speech

T: What does she want? (I forgot . . .)

S: *I forgot what she wanted.*

How does he do it?   How much is it?

Where does he live?   How many do you want?

How do you turn the TV on?

How much time do you need?

How many students are ready?

What does he want?

Where does he work?

Why is he here?

Where is the mail?

What does this word mean?

Why is she sick?

Where is the fire?

How many students are bored?

When does Mary arrive?

Where is he hurt?

How much does it cost?

D. To practice the *past simple tense* and *who* in the subject and object position with *reported* speech

Note: *Be careful of word order. Keep the same word order when* who *is the subject of the clause.*

T: Who is ready? I forgot . . .

S: *I forgot who was ready.*

T: Who(m) does he date? I forgot . . .

S: *I forgot who(m) he dated.*

Who is tired?

Who(m) does he want?

Who(m) does she like?

Who is late?

Who(m) does she visit in the hospital?

Who is early?

Who is sick?

Who(m) does she hate?

Who is on time?

Who(m) do you expect for dinner?

Who(m) do they hear?

Who(m) does he take out?

Who is angry?

Who(m) does she love?

Who is upset?

E. To practice the *past simple tense* with question words in the subject and object position with reported speech

T: What is for sale? I forgot . . .

S: *I forgot what was for sale.*

T: Which book does he need? I forgot . . .

S: *I forgot which book he needed.*

What do you want? I forgot . . .

Which car is yours? I forgot . . .

What does he need? I forgot . . .

What is the price of this book? I forgot . . .

Which movie is the best? I forgot . . .

Which coat is Mary's? I forgot . . .
What time is it? I forgot . . .
Which dress do you like? I forgot . . .
Which is the best wine? I forgot . . .
Which bus does he take? I forgot . . .
What time do you finish work? I forgot . . .
Who is in the hospital? I forgot . . .
What is for dinner? I forgot . . .

Past Continuous Tense

To introduce an action that was *in progress* at some *point* or *period* of time in the past

METHOD

      Draw a time graph on the blackboard; indicate the days (see graph).
      Say the following, marking each *past* action *in progress* by drawing a line across the day to show continued action:

T: Right now, I am teaching this class. Last Saturday, at this time, I was cleaning the house.

       Right now, I am writing on the blackboard. Last Sunday, at this time, I was cooking dinner.

       Right now, I am wearing a red dress. Last Monday, at this time, I was wearing a blue dress.

       Right now, I am standing in front of the class. Last Tuesday, at this time, I was sitting at the desk.

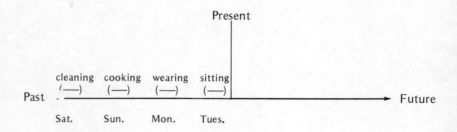

REPEAT

Activity 1: Make a new time graph.

            Ask the students: "What are you doing right now? What were you doing, at this time, last Sunday? etc.

            Mark on the time graph as above.

Activity 2: Make a new time graph; indicate "hours" (e.g., 8—10—12—2—4—6—8).

            Ask the students: "(Yesterday) what were you doing from 8 to 10 a.m.?"
                                        from 10 to 12?
                                        from 12 to 2?
                                        etc.

            Mark on the time graph as above

To introduce *when* and *while* and the *past continuous tense*

METHOD

> Draw a new time graph.
> Say the following, marking each *past continuous* action with a line and
> marking the past action with a vertical arrow.

T: I was taking a bath from 7 to 8. The telephone rang.
When/While I was taking a bath, the telephone rang.

I was getting dressed from 8 to 9. The mail came.
When/While I was getting dressed, the mail came.

I was eating breakfast from 9 to 10. John arrived.
When/While I was eating breakfast, John arrived.

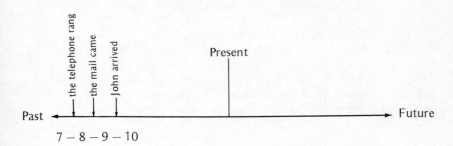

REPEAT

Activity: Make a new time graph.
Ask the students: "What (whom) did you see *while* (*when*) you
were walking to school?"
Mark on the time graph as above.

To introduce the *past continuous tense* and *when* with a *completed* action

METHOD

> Draw a time graph on the blackboard.
> Say the following, marking the *continuous* action with a line and mark-
> ing the *past* action with a vertical arrow.

T: Mary took a long walk yesterday. She saw many people. When Mary
saw the policeman, what was he doing?
mailman
milkman

When Mary saw the policeman, he was directing traffic.

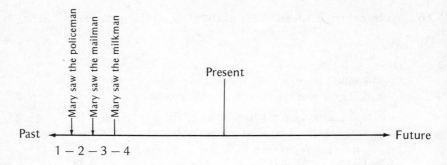

REPEAT

Activity: Make a new time graph.
Ask the students: "What were you doing *when* the bell rang for this class?"
Mark on the time graph as above.

Used to describe an action that was *in progress* at some *point* or *period* of time in the past

DRILL 25   To introduce the *past continuous tense* by contrasting with the *present continuous tense*

A.   List the days of the week on the blackboard. Write the time of the class (e.g., 9 to 11) to the left of the list:

   T: Right now, I'm speaking to the class.

Pointing to each day, go through the list saying:

Last Monday, from (9 to 11), I was giving a test.
Last Tuesday, from (9 to 11), I was correcting homework.
Last Wednesday, from (9 to 11), I was collecting papers.
Last Thursday, from (9 to 11), I was asking questions.
Last Friday, from (9 to 11), I was reading a story to the students.
Last Saturday, from (9 to 11), I was cleaning my apartment.
Last Sunday, from (9 to 11), I was reading the Sunday newspapers.

   Pointing to each day, go through the list and ask the students "What were you doing last   (day) , from (9 to 11)?"
   After each response say: "Right now, you are listening to me. But last   (day)   from (9 to 11), you were _____."
   Have the students ask each other: "What were you doing last   (day)   from (9 to 11)?"

B.   T: What were you doing yesterday from (2 to 4)?

       S1:   *I was studying history .*

   S1 to

       S2:   *Were you studying history yesterday from* (2 to 4)?

       S2:   *No, I wasn't. I was taking a nap .*

   S2 to

       S3:   *Were you taking a nap yesterday from* (2 to 4)?

   Repeat for:

9 to 10 a.m.	8 to 9 a.m.
12 to 1 p.m.	3 to 4 p.m.
8 to 10 p.m.	5 to 6 p.m.
6 to 7 p.m.	7 to 8 a.m.
4 to 10 p.m.	11 to 12 p.m.

DRILL 26   To practice the *past continuous tense* with actions that were *in progress* at a definite *point* in the past

A.   T: What were you doing at 9 o'clock last night?

       S: *At 9 o'clock last night, I was watching TV .*

What were you doing at 10 o'clock last night?

What were you doing at 9 o'clock this morning?

What were you doing at 4 o'clock yesterday afternoon?

What were you doing at 8 o'clock last night?

What were you doing at 6 o'clock yesterday evening?

What were you doing at 10 o'clock last night?

What were you doing at 6 o'clock this morning?

What were you doing at 2 o'clock yesterday afternoon?

What were you doing at 3 o'clock yesterday afternoon?

What were you doing at 1 o'clock this morning?

Note: *Have the students ask each other: "What were you doing at _____ o'clock last night?"*

B.   T: Today is (Monday). What were you doing at this time on Sunday? (wash my hair)

       S1:   *I was washing my hair.*

   S1 to

       S2:   *Were you washing your hair at this time on Sunday?*

       S2:   *Yes, I was.*

       or   *No, I wasn't. I was _____*

watch TV	do my homework
read a book	study English
clean my room	play with my dog

talk to my brother	listen to my records
have dinner	bake cookies
see a film	eat a snack
write letters	dry my hair
talk on the telephone	visit my aunt
take a nap	sit in a cafe

DRILL 27   To practice the *past continuous tense* to emphasize a *continued action* in the past

A.   T: That telephone conversation lasted for 2 hours!   (talk)
S: *We were talking on the telephone for 2 hours!*

That lecture lasted for 2 hours!   (listen to)
That movie lasted for 3 hours!   (watch)
That record played for a half hour!   (listen to)
That test lasted for 2 hours!   (write)
That tape played for 3 hours!   (listen to)
That football game lasted for 4 hours!   (play)
That trip took 6 hours!   (drive)
That flight took 7 hours!   (fly)
That TV program lasted for 2 hours!   (watch)
That tennis match lasted for 3 hours!   (play)

Note: *Do not confuse the* past continuous tense *with the* present perfect continuous tense, *which refers to a long-lasting action that began at some point in the past and continues up to the moment of speaking. The* past continuous *refers to a continued action that* began *and* ended *at definite points in the past.*

B.   T: What were you doing (in the library) so long?   (look for a book)
S: *I was looking for a book.*

in the store   (wait in line to check out)
in the park   (play football)
in school   (talk to the teacher)
in the bedroom   (look for a shirt)
in the garage   (fix the car)
in the office   (type a report)
in the hospital   (have an operation)
in the den   (watch TV)
in the kitchen   (bake cookies)
in the post office   (send a package)
in the bank   (open an account)
in the bar   (talk to a friend)

on the telephone   (talk to my girlfriend)
in the drugstore   (fill a prescription)
in the beauty shop   (get a haircut)
in the police station   (pay a parking ticket)
in the bathroom   (take a bath)

C.   T: Why were you wearing (an apron) this morning?   (bake a cake)
      S: *I was baking a cake this morning.*

tennis shorts   (play tennis)
a bathing suit   (swim)
a suit   (talk to my boss)
a hat   (attend a luncheon)
a raincoat   (walk in the rain)
gloves   (work in the garden)
a black dress   (attend a funeral)
old clothes   (do the housework)
a scarf   (ride a motorcycle)
glasses   (read a book)
pajamas   (stay in bed)
tights   (do my exercises)
a bathrobe   (take a bath)
blue jeans   (fix the car)

D.   T: After class, your teacher asks: "Why were you late for class?"
      S: *I was getting a drink of water.*

In the car, your girlfriend asks: "Why were you late for our date?"
At the dinner table, your (wife) asks: "Why were you late for dinner?"
At the coffee break, your boss asks: "Why were you late for work this morning?"
At the breakfast table, your sister asks: "Why were you late for breakfast this morning?"
At the movie, your friend asks: "Why were you late for the movie?"
In the middle of the month, your landlord asks: "Why were you late with the rent?"

E.   T: Why didn't you finish (painting the room)?   (get tired)
      S: *I was getting tired.*

listening to the lecture   (get bored)
reading the report   (get a headache)
building the snowman   (get cold)
talking to your mother   (get angry)
eating the cake   (get sick)
fixing the car   (get dirty)

    watching that Bergman movie   (get depressed)
    doing that math problem   (get confused)
    cleaning the house   (get lazy)

F.   T: Why are you (late)?   (wait for Mary)
        S: *I'm late because I was waiting for Mary.*
    or   *I was waiting for Mary.*

    tired   (clean the house)
    upset   (worry about my mother)
    quiet   (think about the story)
    cold   (wear only a sweater)
    afraid   (watch a horror movie)
    surprised   (expect someone else)
    worried   (wait for the news)
    hot   (wear a fur coat)
    quiet   (listen to the music)
    nervous   (think about the test)
    drunk   (drink a lot of beer)

G.   T: She didn't know about it because . . .   (travel in Mexico)
        S: *She didn't know about it because she was traveling in Mexico.*

    John was late because . . .   (wait for his brother)
    Mary didn't come because she . . .   (clean the house)
    Bob wasn't home because he . . .   (play in the park)
    I didn't see Jerry because he . . .   (walk the dog)
    I didn't go out because . . .   (do my homework)
    John couldn't go because he . . .   (watch the baby)
    We left early because we . . .   (get tired)
    I woke up because I . . .   (have a bad dream)
    I stopped the car because a child . . .   (sit in the road)
    We couldn't see because it . . .   (get dark)
    She didn't see us because she . . .   (read a book)
    She got up because the baby . . .   (cry)
    She didn't answer the telephone because she . . .   (take a bath)
    John couldn't read the sign because the car . . .   (travel too fast)

DRILL 28   To practice the *past continuous tense* with *always* to emphasize the unusual frequency of the continued action in the past

T: A group of mothers are talking about the things their famous children *were always doing* at an early age.

        Nero's mother   (play with matches)

S: *He was always playing with matches.*

Note: *Use the prompts if necessary. Let the students use their imaginations and think of "famous mothers."*

> Napoleon's mother   (play soldier)
> Mozart's mother   (practice piano)
> Leonardo da Vinci's mother   (invent things)
> Robert Frost's mother   (write poems)
> Pele's mother   (kick footballs)
> Van Gogh's mother   (paint pictures)
> Yves St. Laurent's mother   (make clothes)
> Henry Ford's mother   (play with cars)
> Pablo Casal's mother   (play the cello)
> Shakespeare's mother   (write plays)
> Houdini's mother   (disappear)
> Fellini's mother   (make films)
> Richard Avedon's mother   (take pictures)
> Frank Sinatra's mother   (sing songs)
> Tarzan's mother   (swing in trees)

DRILL 29   To introduce *while* and the *past continuous tense* with an action, also in the past, that interrupted the action in progress

A.   T: Walk across the room, drop an eraser, continue walking. Then, say: "While I was walking across the room, I dropped the eraser."

Ask the students: "What happened while I was walking across the room?"

S: *You dropped the eraser while you were walking across the room.*

Repeat for the following actions:

Walk across the room, drop a pencil, continue walking.
Write on the blackboard, drop the chalk, pick it up, and continue writing.
Start to open the window, bump your head, continue opening the window.
Start to read a story, cough, continue reading the story.
Start to write a sentence on the blackboard, erase a word, continue writing.
Sit down, cross your legs, continue sitting.

Have the students perform actions like pick up a pen, open a book, etc., while they are sitting in their seats. The other students can make statements like: *While John was sitting in his seat, he picked up a pen.*

B.   T: What did you see while you were traveling in Paris?   (Eiffel Tower)

S: *While I was traveling in Paris, I saw the Eiffel Tower.*

Note: *Use prompts if necessary.*

Rome	(St. Peter's)
Berlin	(the Berlin Wall)
Amsterdam	(the windmills)
Madrid	(the Prado)
London	(Big Ben)
Moscow	(the Kremlin)
Egypt	(the pyramids)
India	(the Taj Mahal)
New York	(the Statue of Liberty)
California	(Disneyland)
Panama	(the Panama Canal)

C.   T: What books did you buy while you were shopping at the bookstore?

      S: *While I was shopping at the bookstore, I bought a book on _____ .*

What animals did you see while you were visiting the zoo?
What clothes did you buy while you were shopping at _____ ?
What vegetables did you buy while you were shopping at _____ ?
What pastries did you buy while you were shopping at _____ ?
What music did you listen to while you were buying a record at _____ ?
What shoes did you try on while you were shopping at _____ ?
Who(m) did you visit while you were visiting _New York_ ?
Who(m) did you meet while you were walking in the park?
What exercises did you do while you were doing your homework?
What programs did you see while you were watching TV?

DRILL 30   To introduce *when* in place of *while* with the *past continuous tense*

Note: When *is frequently used with the* past continuous tense *to contrast an action that is "incomplete" with an action (completed) in the simple past tense.*

Repeat the previous drills, using *when* in place of *while*.

A.   Actions: Walk across the room, drop an eraser, continue walking. Then say: "When I was walking across the room, I dropped the eraser."

B.   What did you see *when* you were traveling in Paris?   (Eiffel Tower)
      When I was traveling in Paris, I saw the Eiffel Tower.

C.   What books did you buy *when* you were shopping at the bookstore?
      When I was shopping at the bookstore, I bought a book on _____ .

DRILL 31 To practice *when* and *while* with the *past continuous tense*

A. T: What happened when he was cooking dinner?   (drop the plate)

  S1: *He dropped the plate when he was cooking dinner.*

  S2: *He dropped the plate while he was cooking dinner.*

break the eggs	cut his finger
spill the oil	burn his hand
burn the bread	spill the wine
overcook the potatoes	drop the frying pan
burn the steak	knock over the milk
drop the butter	

B. T: Who(m) did she meet *when* she was traveling in (France)?

  or Who(m) did she meet *while* she was traveling in (France)?

  S1: *She met a Frenchman when she was traveling in France.*

  S2: *She met a Frenchman while she was traveling in France.*

Russia	Egypt
Italy	India
Spain	Ireland
Japan	The United States
Brazil	Iran
Greece	Mexico
Turkey	Nigeria

C. T: What did he buy her *when* he was shopping at the bakery?

  or What did he buy her *while* he was shopping at the bakery?

  S1: *He bought her a cake when he was shopping at the bakery.*

  S2: *He bought her a cake while he was shopping at the bakery.*

shoe store	furniture store
grocery store	liquor store
pharmacy	candy store
hardware store	dairy store
stationery store	magazine stand
bookstore	record shop
appliance store	

DRILL 32 To contrast *when* with a completed action (past tense) with *while/when* with an incompleted action (*past continuous tense*)

A. T: When did he (cut his face)?   (shaving)

  S1: *He cut his face while he was shaving.*

  S2: *He cut his face when he was shaving.*

break his leg	(skiing)
lose his money	(betting at the race track)
snap his wrist	(playing tennis)
almost drown	(water skiing)
slip on his face	(getting out of the bath)
find the book	(clean his room)
buy that mask	(traveling through Africa)
drop the dish	(washing the dishes)
fall asleep	(watching TV)
see her	(walking down the street)
mail the letter	(going to work)
see the house	(driving through the country)
get sick	(eating the cake)

B.　T:　On his way to school this morning, John saw a lot of people. What was the (policeman) doing when John saw him?　　(direct traffic)

　　S:　*The policeman was directing traffic when John saw him.*

mailman	(deliver mail)
grocer	(set up the vegetables)
butcher	(cut steaks)
baker	(sell bread)
milkman	(deliver milk)
bus driver	(pick up people)
newsboy	(deliver papers)

Ask the students to tell you what they saw people doing, saying: "When I saw the principal, he was sitting at his desk."

Repeat, pointing to the use of *when* with the *past simple tense* and with the *past continuous tense.*

　　T:　When did John see the (policeman)?
　　S:　*John saw the policeman when* (or *while*) *he was walking to school.*
　　T:　What was the (policeman) doing when John saw him?
　　S:　*The policeman was directing traffic when John saw him.*

Note:　When *is used with the* past simple tense *(completed action) and with the* past continuous tense *(incompleted action)*. While *is only used with the* past continuous tense *(incomplete action).*

DRILL 33　To contrast *when* with actions occurring at the same moment in the past, and *when* with an action in progress

A.　T:　What happened when the telephone rang?　　(answer it)
　　S1:　*When the telephone rang, I answered it.*

T: What was happening when the telephone rang?   (take a bath)
S2: *When the telephone rang, I was taking a bath.*

What happened when you bought the dress?   (write out a check)
What was happening when you bought the dress?   (shop at Gimbel's)
What happened when you looked out the window?   (see a car accident)
What was happening when you looked out the window?   (baby/cry)
What happened when you heard the news?   (call my husband)
What was happening when you heard the news?   (eat lunch)
What happened when the movie began?   (stop talking)
What was happening when the movie began?   (take my seat)
What happened when he lost his wallet?   (go to the police)
What was happening when he lost his wallet?   (watch a football game)
What happened when your pen ran out of ink?   (borrow my friend's pen)
What was happening when your pen ran out of ink?   (write a letter)
What happened when you dropped the dish?   (break it)
What was happening when you dropped the dish?   (wash the dishes)
What happened when you cleaned the desk?   (find the money)
What was happening when you cleaned the desk?   (look for the money)
What happened when you visited Paris?   (see my friend)
What was happening when you visited Paris?   (write a book)

B.   T: John had a car accident yesterday. What was he driving when he had the accident?
      S: *He was driving a Ford when he had the accident.*
      T: What happened to the car when he had the accident?
      S: *He crashed the car when he had the accident.*

What was he wearing when he had the accident?
What happened to his clothes when he had the accident?

What was he listening to on the radio when he had the accident?
What happened to the radio when he had the accident?

Where was he going when he had the accident?
What happened to his trip when he had the accident?

What was he watching when he had the accident?
What happened to the _____ when he had the accident?

How fast was he traveling when he had the accident?
What happened to the car when he had the accident?

Who(m) was he talking to when he had the accident?
What happened to the passenger when he had the accident?

C.   T: What was happening when your friends arrived?   (read a book)

      S1:   *I was reading a book when my friends arrived.*

      T: What did you do when your friends arrived?

      S2:   *I stopped reading when my friends arrived.*

What was happening when the telephone rang?   (do homework)
What did you do when the telephone rang?

What was happening when you heard a knock on the door?   (watch TV)

What did you do when you heard a knock on the door?

What was happening when you saw John?   (play football)
What did you do when you saw John?

What was happening when John came into the room?   (study English)

What did you do when John came into the room?

What was happening when Betty asked you a question?   (read a magazine)

What did you do when Betty asked you a question?

What was happening when you heard the story?   (eat my lunch)
What did you do when you heard the story?

What was happening when you saw the accident?   (talk to my friend)

What did you do when you saw the accident?

What was happening when you heard the baby cry?   (listen to my records)

What did you do when you heard the baby cry?

What was happening when it started to rain?   (play football)
What did you do when it started to rain?

What was happening when Judy turned on the TV?   (listen to the radio)

What did you do when Judy turned on the TV?

DRILL 34   To practice *while* with two actions occurring *continuously* at the same time in the past

A.   T: Mr. and Mrs. Smith were buying new clothes yesterday. Mr. Smith was trying on clothes in the men's department. At the same time, Mrs. Smith was trying on clothes in the women's department.

      S: *While Mr. Smith was trying on clothes in the men's department, Mrs. Smith was trying on clothes in the women's department.*

Mr. Smith was trying on a shirt, Mrs. Smith a blouse.
Mr. Smith was trying on a tie, Mrs. Smith a scarf.
Mr. Smith was trying on a vest, Mrs. Smith a sweater.
Mr. Smith was trying on a T shirt, Mrs. Smith a slip.
Mr. Smith was trying on a suit, Mrs. Smith a dress.
Mr. Smith was trying on a topcoat, Mrs. Smith a fur coat.
Mr. Smith was trying on a golf cap, Mrs. Smith a flowered hat.
Mr. Smith was trying on a pair of boots, Mrs. Smith a pair of shoes.

B. T: On Sunday, Mr. Smith was relaxing. At the same time, Mrs. Smith was cleaning the house.

  S: *While Mr. Smith was relaxing, Mrs. Smith was cleaning the house.*

Mr. Smith was taking a nap; Mrs. Smith was ironing clothes.
Mr. Smith was reading a newspaper; Mrs. Smith was cooking dinner.
Mr. Smith was looking at a magazine; Mrs. Smith was polishing the silver.
Mr. Smith was watching TV; Mrs. Smith was washing the sheets.
Mr. Smith was talking to his friends; Mrs. Smith was dusting the furniture.
Mr. Smith was writing letters; Mrs. Smith was feeding the baby.
Mr. Smith was planning a vacation; Mrs. Smith was waxing the floor.
Mr. Smith was telephoning his mother; Mrs. Smith was setting the table.
Mr. Smith was practicing his golf swing; Mrs. Smith was sweeping the floor.
Mr. Smith was acting like a king; Mrs. Smith was working like a slave.

C. Have the students ask each other questions, like:

  S1 to
  S2: *What were you doing last night?*
  S2: *I was watching TV last night.*
  S1: *While you were watching TV, I was* (studying English).

Repeat for:

What were you doing last summer?
What were you studying last term?
What were you eating last night?
What TV program were you watching last night at 8 o'clock?
What newspaper were you reading this morning?
What book were you reading last week?

DRILL 35 To practice *just as* with the *past continuous tense*

Note: Just as *is used to indicate that the past action occurred at the moment the* continuous *past action was to begin.*

T: When did the telegram come?   (get home)
S: *The telegram came just as I was getting home.*

> When did the taxi go by?   (get on the bus)
> When did the telephone ring?   (get out of the bath)
> When did the ship pull out?   (arrive at the port)
> When did the train arrive?   (reach the station)
> When did he get sick?   (leave for the trip)
> When did the girl fall?   (get off the horse)
> When did the snow start?   (leave the house)
> When did the mail arrive?   (walk to the door)
> When did you meet him?   (leave the party)
> When did you run out of ink?   (start the letter)
> When did you see the telegram?   (leave the house)
> When did John stop by?   (take a bath)
> When did the battery die out?   (start the motor)
> When did you run out of thread?   (start the dress)

DRILL 36   To practice *just* with the *past continuous tense*

T: I just started my homework.   (the telephone rang)
S: *I was just starting my homework when the telephone rang.*

> the telegram arrived   the dog barked
> the lights went out   the visitors came
> the man knocked on the door   the flowers arrived
> the groceries arrived   the pen ran out of ink
> the teakettle whistled

DRILL 37   To contrast *just* and *just as* with the *past continuous tense*

T: Just as I was starting my homework, the telephone rang.
S: *I was just starting my homework when the telephone rang.*

> Just as I was turning on the TV, John came over.
> Just as I was getting into the bath, Bob knocked on the door.
> Just as I was locking the door, George came home.
> Just as I was leaving the hospital, the doctor arrived.
> Just as I was setting the table, the guests came.
> Just as I was entering the station, the train pulled out.
> Just as I was getting into my seat, the movie started.
> Just as I was choosing the wine, the waiter appeared.
> Just as I was teaching the lesson, the principal walked in.
> Just as I was turning on the TV, the program ended.

DRILL 38   To practice the *past continuous tense* with *verbs of anticipation* to express unfulfilled actions

Note: *Although normally used with the* past simple tense, *verbs of anticipation are often used with the* past continuous tense. *When used in the* past simple *or* past continuous tenses, *and when referring to the speaker, these verbs carry a meaning of "I wanted to, but didn't." "Hope to," "plan to," and "intend to" are often used interchangeably. However, the students should be familiar with the distinctions in meaning.*

Example: hope to: "I hope to see you soon." (a real possibility—we're in the same business.)

intend to: "I intend to see you soon." (you need his advice on business—you'll have to see him sometime soon.)

plan to: "I plan to see you soon." (you ask your secretary to arrange a definite luncheon date with him.)

Example: hope to: "I hope to visit Spain." (You're young and have lots of time ahead.)

intend to: "I intend to visit Spain." (You have a month's vacation next summer)

plan to: "I plan to visit Spain." (You have the tickets in your pocket.)

A.   T: I forgot to bring my homework. (Note: I didn't bring it.) (bring)

S: *I was planning to bring my homework (but I didn't).*

I missed the 10 o'clock flight.   (take)
I forgot to bring the book.   (bring)
I couldn't get to the museum.   (go)
I didn't remember to call Bill.   (telephone)
I left the house late.   (leave early)
I got to bed after midnight.   (go before midnight)
I forgot to invite John to the party.   (invite)
I came to the party early.   (come late)
I forgot to buy the wine.   (pick up)
I missed the first boat.   (take)
I wanted to study for the test.   (study)
I met Mary for lunch at 2:30.   (meet her at 2)
I took the bus.   (take the train)

B.   Repeat A, using *intend to* in place of *plan to*

T: I forgot to bring my homework.   (bring)
S: *I was intending to bring my homework (but I didn't).*

C.   Repeat A, using *hope to* in place of *plan to*

T: I forgot to bring my homework.   (bring)

S: *I was hoping to bring my homework (but I didn't).*

D.   To practice the *past continuous tense* with *expect*

Note: *When* expect *is used in the* past continuous tense, *it carries the meaning of "anticipating" an event that the speaker has good reason to believe will happen. For example, when we say "Mary is expecting a baby in August," although very idiomatic, we are referring to the fact that she is carrying a child, not just "hoping," "planning," or "intending" to have a child in August.*

T: John is telling his friend about his Christmas (or birthday) presents: "My aunt always gives me a book."

S: *I was expecting a book, but I got money from my aunt.*

My sister always gives me a shirt.

My mother always gives me a sweater.

My brother always gives me a record.

My girlfriend always gives me cologne.

My uncle always gives me handkerchiefs.

My aunt always gives me a hat.

My cousin always gives me a scarf.

My grandmother always gives me a tie.

My grandfather always gives me a belt.

E.   To practice *going to* to express unfulfilled past action

T: John intended to study for the test. (Note: but he didn't.)

S: *John was going to study for the test (but he didn't).*

They intended to sell the car.

She intended to get married last month.

We intended to visit them last week.

I intended to invite John to the party.

He intended to go to the University.

I intended to call you last night.

We intended to buy a new house.

The students intended to study for the test.

She intended to send her a birthday card.

He intended to take an early flight.

They intended to buy tickets for the opera.

He intended to see that play.

She intended to save money.

I intended to send him a letter.

F. To practice the *past continuous tense* to express unfulfilled actions

   T: When is John arriving?   (Thursday)
   S: *He was arriving on Thursday, but now he isn't.*

What flight are you taking?   (Pan Am)
Which play is he seeing?   (Shakespearian play)
When are you meeting Mary?   (at 2 o'clock)
Where is he staying?   (Hilton)
Where are you meeting the girls?   (at the library)
When are you sending the letter?   (this afternoon)
What is she serving for dinner?   (fish)
Which night are you having the party?   (Saturday)
What kind of car is he buying?   (Ford)
Which movie are you seeing?   (the Italian movie)
Where are you eating lunch?   (the French restaurant)
Which magazine is she buying?   (*Vogue*)
How many people are you inviting to the party?   (50)
Which dress is she wearing to the party?   (the red one)
What time are you leaving?   (at 10 o'clock)
What are you having for lunch?   (a pizza)

Present Perfect Tense

To introduce an action begun in the past and continuing *up to* and probably *into* the future

METHOD

      Draw a time graph on the blackboard.

      Say the following, marking the *start* of a past action with an x; draw a *solid* line from the x across the present and continue with a *dotted* line into the future.

T: I started teaching this class in September. (I am still teaching this class, and I plan to continue teaching this class.)

      Up to now, I have given 5 tests.

                        corrected 200 papers

                        shown 4 movies

                        taught 15 units of the book

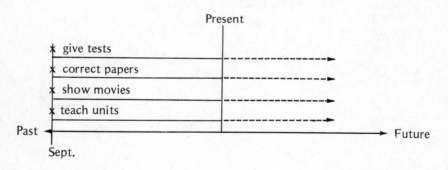

REPEAT

Activity 1: Make a new time graph.

            Ask the students: "How many tests   have we had up to now?

                                    drills

                                    holidays

                                    report cards

                                    etc.

            (Are we still taking tests? Do we plan to continue taking tests?)

            Mark on the time graph as above.

Activity 2: Make a new time graph. (Mark "last month"—Dec.?—instead of Sept.)

Ask the students: "How many books have you read   since
    December?"   plays have you seen
                                  magazines have you bought
                                  museums have you visited
Mark on the time graph as above.

Used to express the time from some moment in the past to the present moment of speaking

Note: *This tense is frequently used in English, although many languages do not have a comparable tense.*

DRILL 39   To contrast the *present perfect tense* with the *past simple tense*

A.   T: (read that book)
     S1: *When did you read that book?*
     S2: *I read it last week.*
   S2 to
     S3: *Have you read that book?*
     S3: *Yes, I read it last year.*

see that movie	travel to Paris
hear that record	learn that poem
take that test	take that new train
visit that museum	get your driver's license
go to New York	read that new magazine

Note: *Instead of using "that book" or "that movie," substitute the name of a book or film familiar to the students.*

B.   T: Have you (eaten breakfast) today?
     S: *Yes, I have. I ate breakfast an hour ago.*

read the newspaper	bought the paper
heard the news	taken a bath
walked the dog	ironed the clothes
fixed dinner	found the money
studied for the test	called Judy
played the new record	written the letter
taken the exam	gone to the bookstore
done your homework	mailed the letter
listened to the news	swept the floor
turned off the light	seen Aunt Anna

C.   T: Mary (ate 3 candy bars) yesterday.

         S1:   *She's eaten three today and it's only 1 o'clock.*

    S1 to

         S2:   *How many candy bars have you eaten today?*

         S2:   *I've eaten one today.*

         or   *I haven't eaten any today.*

drank 4 cokes	took 2 tests
wrote 3 letters	made 6 telephone calls
read 4 newspapers	watched 5 TV programs
saw 2 movies	listened to 8 records
took 4 taxis	ate 2 apples
played 3 sets of tennis	made 5 sandwiches
bought 4 magazines	

D.   T: John eats three meals every day.

         S1:   *He ate three meals yesterday.*

         S2:   *He's eaten three meals (so far) today.*

John plays tennis 2 hours every day.

My secretary types 25 pages every day.

We study 5 hours every day.

My mother cooks 3 meals every day.

My father works 8 hours every day.

The children play football 3 hours every day.

My teacher teaches 5 hours every day.

The mailman walks 6 miles every day.

We practice drills 2 hours every day.

I comb my hair 10 times every day.

The doctor visits 15 people every day.

Our teacher gives 2 tests every day.

DRILL 40   To use students' experiences to practice the present perfect tense

A.   T: We started this class in (September).

             How many (tests) have we had up to now?

       S: *We've had _____ tests up to now.*

lessons	language laboratory periods
exercises	teachers
examinations	class hours
drills	homework assignments
field trips	holidays
movies	parties

B.   T: How many times have you (brushed your teeth) today?
    S1:   *I've brushed my teeth _____ times today.*
  S1 to
    S2:   *How many times have you brushed your teeth today?*
    S2:   *I've brushed my teeth _____ times today.*
       etc.

      washed your hair   telephoned your girlfriend
      combed your hair   taken the bus
      taken a shower   gone for a drink of water
      coughed   seen the principal
      talked to your friends

C.   T: How many cars have you driven so far?
    S1:   *I've driven _____ cars so far.*
  S1 to
    S2:   *How many cars have you driven so far?*
    S2:   *I've driven _____ cars so far.*
       etc.

How many languages have you learned so far?
Where have you traveled in Europe so far?
Who(m) have you visited in (New York) so far?
What programs have you seen on TV so far?
How many plays have you seen so far?
How many times have you cut your hair so far?
How often have you seen the dentist so far?
How many hours have you studied so far?
How many meals have you eaten so far?
How much wine have you drunk so far?
How many cigarettes have you smoked so far?
How often have you changed your hair style so far?
Where have you eaten so far?
How much ice cream have you eaten so far?
What kind of music have you heard so far?
How much money have you spent so far?
How many girls have you dated so far?
How many nightclubs have you gone to so far?
How many cars have you bought so far?

D.   T: How many movies have you seen this month?
    S1:   *I've seen _____ movies this month.*
  S1 to
    S2:   *How many movies have you seen this month?*
    S2:   *I've seen _____ movies this month.*
       etc.

How many lessons have you done this week?
How often have you taken a vacation this year?
How much ice cream have you eaten this week?
How many magazines have you read this week?
Which books have you read this year?
How many phone calls have you made this week?
How many letters have you written this month?
How many times have you worn that sweater this week?
How many trips have you taken this year?
Which newspapers have you read this week?
How many telegrams have you sent this year?
What clothes have you bought this month?
How many times have you gotten a cold this year?
How often have you had the flu this year?
How many parties have you given this year?
How many parties have you gone to this year?
How often have you shopped for food this week?
How many times have you taken a test this week?

E. T: How many times have you visited (Paris)?
     S: *I've visited Paris three times* (and will probably visit Paris again).

New York	Madrid
Athens	Istanbul
Rome	Mexico City
London	Chicago
Zurich	

Note: *The names of the cities above can be changed to local places and areas more familiar to the students.*

F. T: Can you drive a car?
     S: *Yes, I've driven a car before (now).*
  or   *No, I haven't driven a car before (now).*
  (if yes)
     T: When did you learn to drive a car?
     S: *I learned to drive a car when I was 16 or in 19_____ .*

play tennis	play football
type	ski
take dictation	play piano
sew	cook Chinese food
knit	write poetry
fix a flat tire	paint
repair a radio	ride a bicycle

DRILL 41   To practice the *present perfect tense* with *for* and *since*

A.   T: I'm a member of that club. I joined last year.
      S1:   *I've been a member of that club for a year.*
      S2:   *I've been a member of that club since 19 _____ .*

I'm a student at the University. I entered 2 years ago.
I'm a cook at the hotel. I started 4 years ago.
I'm a soldier. I joined the Army 3 years ago.
I'm a farmer. I bought a farm 10 years ago.
I'm a reporter for the *New York Times.* I got the job a year ago.
I'm a lawyer. I joined that firm 5 years ago.
I'm a businessman. I bought the store 25 years ago.
I'm a widow. My husband died 3 years ago.
I'm a married man. I got married 10 years ago.
I'm a congressman. I got elected 2 years ago.
I'm a policeman. I joined the force 5 years ago.
I'm a taxi driver. I got my license 10 years ago.

B.   T: I stopped smoking 2 years ago.
       S: *I haven't smoked for 2 years.*

driving 10 years ago
eating candy a month ago
seeing him last week
working late 6 months ago
taking taxis 3 months ago
working last month
making business trips 3 years ago
using my fur coat 2 months ago
sending Christmas cards 5 years ago
studying French 2 months ago
drinking beer last month
staying up late 3 months ago
getting a haircut last year
buying that magazine 3 weeks ago
reading the newspaper last week

Repeat, using *since.*

    T: I stopped smoking 2 years ago.
    S: *I haven't smoked since 19 _____ .*

C.   T: The last time I saw him was 3 days ago.
       S: *I haven't seen him for 3 days.*

The last time John got a haircut was 6 months ago.
The last time Mary wrote her parents was 3 weeks ago.

The last time I had a cup of coffee was 8 hours ago.
The last time the children came over for lunch was a week ago.
The last time the Browns visited was 2 years ago.
The last time I missed the bus was a year ago.
The last time Jim failed a test was 2 months ago.
The last time we had dinner with you was 4 months ago.
The last time George cooked dinner was 6 nights ago.
The last time they visited us was 2 years ago.
The last time I gave her money was in August.
The last time I worked was 3 years ago.
The last time Greg sent me a postcard was 3 years ago.
The last time I took a taxi was last Friday.
The last time we saw Jim was on Christmas Day.
The last time I got a present from Bill was on my birthday.
The last time he water-skied was in the summer.
The last time they borrowed a book was in March.
The last time I took a test was last week.

Repeat, using *since.*

T: The last time I saw him was 3 days ago.
S: *I haven't seen him since (Monday).*

D. T: John gave up drinking last year.
S1: *John hasn't had a drink for a year.*
S2: *John hasn't had a drink since 19 _____ .*

Mary gave up smoking last month.
Bill gave up eating candy last week.
Barbara gave up giving parties last year.
Mrs. Smith gave up drinking coffee last month.
John gave up dating last week.
Margaret gave up eating bread last month.
Susan gave up drinking coke last week.
Mrs. Jones gave up taking sleeping pills last year.
Bob gave up betting on horses last year.   (make a bet)
Bill gave up playing golf last month.   (play a game of golf)
Bob gave up jogging last week.   (jog)
Judy gave up dancing 10 years ago.   (dance)
Mary gave up singing 5 years ago.   (sing)
Jane gave up watching the late movie last year.   (see)
Jim gave up driving sports cars 4 years ago.   (drive)
Tom gave up skiing 3 years ago.   (ski)
Michael gave up hunting last year.   (hunt)

E. T: Have you seen John recently?   (3 months)
　　S1: *I haven't seen him for 3 months.*
　　T: (March)
　　S2: *I haven't seen him since March.*

read a good book	watched TV
a year	3 nights
19_____	(Thursday)
got a letter from Mark	dyed your hair
2 months	2 years
(October)	19_____
bought a newspaper	heard from Judy
a week	2 months
(Sunday)	(February)
gone to any good movies	received your bank statement
a month	3 weeks
(a month ago)	(September 5)
lost any books	gone to the zoo
2 weeks	six months
(2 weeks ago)	the summer
gone to that restaurant	gotten any mail
a month	2 days
(June)	(2 days ago)

DRILL 42　To practice the *present perfect tense* with *still*

A. T: John turned the (light) on 10 minutes ago. It's still on.
　　S: *John has turned the light on.*

TV	air conditioner
iron	heater
radio	washing machine
stove	dishwasher
stereo	hair dryer
tape recorder	toaster

B. T: John's mother asked him to (clean his room) an hour ago. He forgot.
　　S: *He still hasn't cleaned his room.*

wash the dishes	shine his shoes
take out the garbage	iron his shirt
wash the car	do his homework
walk the dog	write his aunt a thank you note
take a bath	water the plants
pick up his clothes	go to the store

C. **T:** When the mayor was elected last year, he promised to do many things. He promised to fix the roads.

S: *He still hasn't fixed the roads.*

build new schools	lower the taxes
hire more policemen	build more homes for the poor
give raises to the teachers	stop crime
clean the streets	build new hospitals
build more parks	get rid of the old politicians
improve public transportation	

DRILL 43   To practice the *present perfect tense* with *ever* and *never*

A. **T:** Have you ever seen a(n)   (elephant)?

S1: *Yes, I saw one in 19_____ .*

S2: *No, I never have.*

camel	kangaroo
zebra	lion
koala bear	anteater
cobra	tiger
gorilla	giraffe
tarantula	martian

B. **T:** (work on a farm)

S1: *Have you ever worked on a farm?*

S2: *Yes, I worked on a farm in 19_____.*

S3: *No, I've never worked on a farm.*

S4: *I never have.*

travel to Africa	type a letter
visit the Taj Mahal	feed a baby
climb Mt. Everest	smoke a cigar
act in a play	ride a horse
write a song	travel in space
bake a cake	vote in an election
write a book	eat raw fish
throw a pot	ride a camel
paint a portrait	sail a boat
take a photograph	

DRILL 44   To practice the *present perfect tense* with *because*

T: She knows the ending.   (see the movie before)
S: *She knows the ending because she's seen the movie.*

    She won't eat the dessert.   (gain 10 pounds)
    He can't get in.   (lock the door)
    He won't take the car.   (not fix the flat tire)
    She has the money.   (cash her paycheck)
    She doesn't know his address.   (lose her address book)
    She can't do her homework.   (forgot her book)
    He's not going to New York.   (miss the plane)
    He can't read the newspaper.   (lose his glasses)
    She can't tell the time.   (break her watch)
    He won't go skiing.   (catch a cold)
    She can't make the cake.   (run out of flour)
    He won't have the apartment next year.   (not sign the lease)
    He can show you how to fix it.   (do it before)
    She can't sew the dress.   (break her needle)

DRILL 45   To practice the *present perfect tense* with *just* to express the *recency* of the completed action

A.   T: Will you (do your homework) now?
      S: *I've just done it!*

start the dinner	turn off the TV
turn on the light	pick up the books
shut off the air conditioner	mail those letters
make the beds	sweep the floor
clean the house	iron those shirts
walk the dog	clean up your room
take out the garbage	

B.   T: Judy typed the letter a few minutes ago.
      S: *She's just typed the letter.*

    They got married last Saturday.
    Janet left a few moments ago.
    I passed my driving test yesterday.
    John got back from his vacation last night.
    I picked up the mail this morning.
    The teacher told us our grades this morning.
    She came the day before yesterday.
    The light went off a second ago.
    I wrote to him last night.
    Bill made the reservations yesterday.

The children arrived a short time ago.
The bus pulled in a few moments ago.
You missed him by a second.
She took a shower an hour ago.
Michael cut his hair this afternoon.
The package arrived a little while ago.
I went to London only a week ago.
John caught the flu this weekend.

C. T: Have you seen any good movies lately?
  S: *I've just seen* _____ .

Have you read any good books lately?
Have you met any interesting people lately?
Have you read any good stories lately?
Have you heard any good jokes lately?
Have you gone to any good restaurants lately?
Have you seen any good plays lately?
Have you listened to any good records lately?
Have you seen any good TV programs lately?
Have you gone to any good football games lately?
Have you taken any easy tests lately?
Have you bought any new clothes lately?

DRILL 46   To practice the *present perfect tense* with *already* and *yet*

Note: *"Already" is used to show that the action was completed at the moment of speaking.*

A. T: Has anyone started the (lesson) yet?
  S1: *Yes, we've already started it.*
  S2: *No, we haven't started it yet.*

the fire	the game
the wash	the program
the dishes	the class
the book	the exercises
the homework	the lecture
the meeting	the movie
the story	the slides

B. T: Have you (done your homework) yet?
  S: *I've already done it, but John hasn't done his homework yet.*

cleaned your room	read your book
made your bed	listened to your records
studied your lesson	ironed your clothes

taken your bath
sent out your Christmas cards
cut your nails
shined your shoes
brushed your teeth
made your phone calls

paid your bills
tried on your new shoes
driven your new car
watered your plants
passed in your paper
finished the test

C.   T: There's a new movie in town.   (see)
     S1:   *Have you seen it yet?*
     S2:   *I've already seen it.*
     S3:   *I haven't seen it yet.*

student in class   (meet)
airplane flying to Paris   (take)
magazine out   (buy)
program on TV   (watch)
trip to London   (take)
record out   (hear)
toothpaste out   (buy)
car out   (ride in)
lipstick out   (use)
house for sale   (see)

DRILL 47   To practice the *present perfect tense* with *been* in place of some past verbs

A.   T: John went to Europe last year.
   S1 to
     S2:   *Have you ever been to Europe?*
     S2:   *Yes, I have. I went to Europe in 19_____.*
     or   *No, I never have.*

Bob visited the National Museum last week.
Judy traveled in Mexico last summer.
John went in the army last year.
Bill was late to class this morning.
Jack was in jail last year.
Jane had dinner at Sardi's.
Steve went to the Olympics last year.
Robert was in the Navy two years ago.
Betty saw the opera last night.
Mary went in the hospital for an operation.
Michael got into trouble with the police.
John visited Paris last month.

B. T: John started to be late for class 3 days ago.
S1: *He's been late for class for 3 days.*
S2: *He's been late for class since Thursday.*

They went to Spain a month ago.
The children went to bed 10 minutes ago.
Jerry got sick a week ago.
We got here at 2 o'clock.
She became a teacher last year.
The policeman went on duty at 8 o'clock.
It got cold last Thursday.
John fell asleep at 11 o'clock.
The air conditioner went on this morning.
She got depressed last week.
My sister went away last month.
It got sunny at 10 o'clock.
The elevator went out of order this morning.
The weather turned cool at noon.
We get busy at 3 o'clock.
Betty went to the hospital last Thursday.
The store got busy at 4 o'clock.
I got tired at 10 o'clock.
It got quiet this morning.
Jim became a doctor in 19 _____ .

Present Perfect Continuous

To introduce the *present perfect continuous* to express a continuous and uninterrupted action, begun in the past, and continuing *up to* and *into* the future

METHOD

Draw a time graph on the blackboard.

Say the following, marking the start of a past action with an x; draw a solid line of x's, from that point across to the present, and continue with a dotted line into the future.

T: I started walking in 19 _____ .
talking
reading
working

(I am still walking and I plan to continue walking.)

I have *been* walking since 19_____ .
talking
reading
working

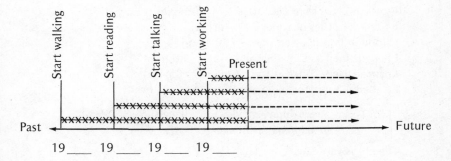

REPEAT

Activity 1: Make a new time graph.
Ask the students: "When did you start walking ?"
talking
reading
studying
(Are you still _____ ? Do you plan to continue _____ ?)
Mark on the time graph as above.

Activity 2: Make a new time graph.
Ask the students: "When did you start studying English?"
John has *been* studying English since 19 _____ .
Mark on the time graph as above.

Used to express the time from some moment in the past to the present moment of speaking when *continuous* action and *recency* are emphasized

DRILL 48   To emphasize continuous action

A.   T: I cleaned every room in the house.   (clean)
      S: *I've been cleaning for hours!*

I couldn't find a taxi.   (walk)
I played all my old records.   (listen to records)
I read every page of the newspaper.   (read)
I wrote 10 letters.   (write)
I typed 50 pages.   (type)
I washed 4 loads of clothes.   (wash)
I painted every room in the house.   (paint)
I addressed 200 Christmas cards.   (address/them)
I made 3 dresses.   (sew)
I smoked 2 packs of cigarettes.   (smoke)
I drank 2 bottles of wine.   (drink)
I stood in line all afternoon.   (stand)
I bought the food for the week.   (shop)
I danced every dance at the party.   (dance)
I waited 4 hours for the plane to arrive.   (wait)

B.   T: This is a very funny movie.   (laugh)
      S: *I've been laughing for hours.*

The bus is very late.   (stand)
The alarm clock is broken.   (sleep)
The movie is very long.   (sit)
The disco music is great!   (dance)
The test is tomorrow.   (study)
The food is delicious.   (eat)
John is very late.   (worry)
The book is very sad.   (cry)
This recipe for chicken is very difficult.   (cook)
This report is very long.   (type)

DRILL 49   To practice *ever since* with the *present perfect continuous tense*

Note: *The* present perfect continuous tense *is used instead of the* present perfect simple tense *when* continuity *of the action is emphasized.*

T: John sold his first story. Then, he began writing for a living.
S: *Ever since he sold his first story, John has been writing for a living.*
or   *John has been writing for a living ever since he sold his first story.*

Bob joined the sports club. Then, he began playing football every Saturday.
Betty bought a sewing machine. Then, she began making her own clothes.
Mary won $10,000 in the contest. Then, she began spending a lot of money.
Bill went to see the doctor. Then, he began dieting.
Tom got a new car. Then, he began driving to work.
Susan got a dog. Then, she began going to the park every day.
David's wife died. Then, he began drinking a lot.
John broke his TV. Then, he began listening to the radio.
Jim had a car accident. Then, he began taking the bus to work.
Cathy got a new washing machine. Then, she began washing her own clothes.
Sharon got Jim's letter. Then, she began crying all the time.
Judy hurt her leg. Then, she began exercising.
Bob got the flu. Then, he began taking vitamins.

DRILL 50   To practice the *present perfect continuous tense* with *for* and *since*

A.   T: She started living in (Paris) in 1975. She's still there.
S1:   *She's been living in Paris since 1975.*
S2:   *She's been living in Paris for _____ years.*

London/last year	Sydney/for ages
Nairobi/before the war	Cairo/after the war
Brussels/a year ago	Copenhagen/three years ago
New York/in 1960	Chicago/last summer
Mexico City/two years ago	Athens/last winter
Rio de Janeiro/in 1970	

B.   T: He began cleaning his room an hour ago and he hasn't finished yet.
S1:   *He's been cleaning his room for an hour.*
S2:   *He's been cleaning his room since _____ o'clock.*

He began fixing the radio at 2 o'clock and he hasn't finished yet.
He began reading that magazine 3 hours ago and he hasn't finished yet.
He began watching TV 2 hours ago and he hasn't finished yet.
He began studying for the test this morning and he hasn't finished yet.
He began talking on the telephone an hour ago and he hasn't finished yet.
He began eating his lunch at noon and he hasn't finished yet.
He began writing a letter 2 hours ago and he hasn't finished yet.
He began washing his clothes at 2 o'clock and he hasn't finished yet.
He began ironing his shirts this morning and he hasn't finished yet.
He began taking pictures 2 hours ago and he hasn't finished yet.
He began dressing a half hour ago and he hasn't finished yet.
He began taking the test this morning and he hasn't finished yet.
He began decorating the room an hour ago and he hasn't finished yet.
He began painting the walls this afternoon and he hasn't finished yet.
He began listening to records 2 hours ago and he hasn't finished yet.
He began studying at the university in 1970 and he hasn't finished yet.

C. To use students' experiences to practice the *present perfect continuous tense*

T: How long have you been studying English?
S1: *I've been studying English for _____ years.*
or *I've been studying English since 19 _____ .*
S1 to
S2: *How long have you been studying English?*
      etc.

How long have you been living at your present address?
How long have you been watching TV?
How long have you been driving a car?
How long have you been using that pen?
How long have you been wearing those shoes?
How long have you been growing that beard?
How long have you been smoking that brand of cigarettes?
How long have you been carrying that pocketbook?
How long have you been using that lipstick?
How long have you been dating that girl?
How long have you been seeing that doctor?
How long have you been going to that restaurant?
How long have you been paying taxes?
How long have you been going to that bank?
How long have you been using that book bag?
How long have you been drinking coke?

DRILL 51 To contrast the *present perfect,* the *past,* and the *present perfect continuous tenses*

T: How many languages have you studied so far?
S1: *I've studied_____languages so far.*
T: How long have you been studying English?
S2: *I've been studying English for _____ years.*
or *I've been studying English since 19_____.*
T: When did you start studying English?
S3: *I started studying English in 19_____ .*

How many different restaurants have you gone to so far this year?
How long have you been eating in this restaurant?
When did you start eating here?

How many books have you read this year?
How long have you been reading that book?
When did you start reading that book?

How many cokes have you had today?
How long have you been drinking coke?
When did you start drinking coke?

How many concerts have you given this year?
How long have you been practicing for this concert?
When did you start practicing for this concert?

How many books have you written this year?
How long have you been writing this book?
When did you start writing this book?

How many tennis lessons have you had so far?
How long have you been taking tennis lessons?
When did you start taking tennis lessons?

How many cigarettes have you smoked today?
How long have you been smoking?
When did you start smoking?

How many visits to the doctor have you made this year?
How long have you been visiting the doctor?
When did you start visiting the doctor?

How many pictures have you taken this month?
How long have you been taking pictures?
When did you start taking pictures?

How many portraits have you painted this year?
How long have you been painting portraits?
When did you start painting portraits?

How many letters have you typed so far today?
How long have you been typing?
When did you start typing?

How many records have you bought this year?
How long have you been buying records?
When did you start buying records?

How many TV programs have you watched this week?
How long have you been watching TV?
When did you start watching TV?

How many miles have you driven so far? (Note: check the odometer!)
How long have you been driving your new car?
When did you start driving?

DRILL 52   To practice the *present perfect continuous tense* with *because*
to emphasize the *recency* of the continuous action in the past

Note: *The* past continuous tense *is used after* because *when the action*
began *and* ended *at definite points in the past. The* present perfect continuous
tense *is used after* because *when the action began at a definite point in the
past and continues to the* moment of speaking.

T: Why is she tired?   (work very hard)
S: *She's tired because she's been working very hard.*

Why do your eyes hurt?   (watch TV)
Why is your skin red?   (scratch)
Why are your eyes burning?   (peel onions)
Why is your hair wet?   (swim)
Why is your room a mess?   (look for a book)
Why is the iron hot?   (iron a shirt)
Why are you sweating?   (do my exercises)
Why is the camera on the table?   (take photographs)
Why are the records out?   (listen to some music)
Why is the ladder up?   (paint the ceiling)
Why is the sewing machine out?   (sew a dress)
Why is the furniture outside?   (wax the floors)
Why are you crying?   (read a sad story)

DRILL 53   To practice the *present perfect continuous tense* with *who* to
emphasize the recency of a continuous action in the past

T: The cover is off the cookie jar.   (eat)
S: *Who's been eating the cookies?*

The magazines are on the floor.   (read)
The iron is on.   (iron)
The milk is boiling over.   (boil)
The cake is burning.   (bake)
The car is out of the garage.   (drive)
The oven is on.   (use)
The cap is off the toothpaste.   (brush/teeth)
The bed is a mess.   (sleep)
The TV is on.   (watch)
The bathtub is dirty.   (take a bath)
The radio is on.   (listen to)
The beer is gone.   (drink)
The stereo is on.   (play/records)
The sewing machine is out.   (sew)
The clothes are in the dryer.   (do a wash)
The Monopoly game is on the floor.   (play)
Pots and pans are in the sink.   (cook)
The room is full of smoke.   (smoke)
The mail is open.   (read)

DRILL 54   To practice *short* answers with the *past, present perfect,* and *present perfect continuous tenses*

T: Have you seen my book?
S1:   *No, I haven't.*
S2:   *Yes, I have. I saw it* (on the table).
T: Did you visit her last week?
S1:   *No, I didn't.*
S2:   *Yes, I did. I visited her* (last Monday).
T: Have you been studying long?
S1:   *No, I haven't.*
S2:   *Yes, I have. I've been studying* (for 2 hours/since 11 o'clock).

Have you seen that movie before?
Have you been reading?
Did you take that book?
Have you written the letter?
Did you mail the letter?
Have you been writing long?
Did you stop smoking?
Have you been smoking just now?
Have you seen the Eiffel Tower?
Has John arrived?

Did he call?
Have we met you before?
Did you wait long?
Has she written you?
Did the children hear the record?
Have you been waiting long?
Did you get the flu?
Have you been sick this year?
Did you lock the door?
Have they served dinner yet?
Did the dog bark a moment ago?
Have you been studying English very long?
Did Janet go to the party?
Has she been a teacher long?
Did John win the race?
Have you read that book?
Did they telephone?
Has she been studying long?
Did you leave the house last night?
Has the baby been crying long?
Did the flowers arrive?
Have you started the test yet?
Have you been sleeping?
Did they leave for the airport on time?
Have they been away long?
Has she seen the film?

Past Perfect Tense

To introduce the *past perfect tense* with a past action that occurred *before* another past action

METHOD

Draw a time graph on the blackboard; mark the times (see graph).
Say the following, marking an x for the past action. Draw a curved
arrow from the first past action to the second; from the second to
the third, etc.

T: At 7:00, I got up.
      7:05, I took a shower.
      7:15, I got dressed.
      7:30, I ate breakfast.
      8:00, I went to school.

After I had gotten up, I took a shower.
After I had taken a shower, I got dressed.
After I had gotten dressed, I ate breakfast.
After I had eaten breakfast, I went to school.

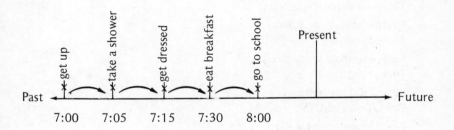

REPEAT

Activity 1: Make a new time graph. (Mark in "times")
              Ask the students: "This morning, what did you do first?
                                                            second?
                                                            third?
                                                            fourth?

              After (John) had _____ , he_____ .
              Mark on the time graph as above.

Activity 2: Make a new time graph.

Ask the students: Mary baked a cake yesterday.

What did she do first?

second?

third?

fourth?

After she had _____ , she _____ .

Mark on the time graph as above.

Used to express an action that occurred *before* another action in the past

DRILL 55   To practice the *past perfect tense* with *when* and *as soon as* to show that the first action occurred *before* the second action

T: First, I ate dinner.

Then, I did the dishes.

S1:   *When I had eaten dinner, I did the dishes.*

S2:   *As soon as I had eaten dinner, I did the dishes.*

First, I made the reservations.

Then, I asked her to dinner.

First, I ordered the wine.

Then, I ordered the dinner.

First, I washed the floor.

Then, I waxed it.

First, I smoked the cigarette.

Then, I put it out.

First, I did my homework.

Then, I watched TV.

First, I painted the walls.

Then, I hung the pictures.

First, I washed the clothes.

Then, I put them in the dryer.

First, I bought Mary a present.

Then, I wrapped it.

First, I drove 10 miles.

Then, I ran out of gas.

First, I mixed the cake.

Then, I put it in the oven.

First, I fed the dog.

Then, I took him for a walk.

First, I bought some stamps.
Then, I mailed the letter.
First, I finished the research for the paper.
Then, I wrote it.
First, I looked up her number in the telephone book.
Then, I called her.
First, I paid the bill.
Then, I got a receipt.

DRILL 56 To contrast *when* with the *past perfect tense* and *when* with the *past tense* (both actions occured *at the same time* in the past)

T: I ate my breakfast. I went to school.
S: *When I had eaten my breakfast, I went to school.*
T: The bullet hit him. He died instantly.
S: *When the bullet hit him, he died instantly.*
or *As soon as the bullet hit him, he died.*
Note: The moment *the bullet hit him, he died.*

I dropped the plate. I broke it.
I learned to dance. I entered a dance contest.
He stood up. He bumped his head.
John slipped. He broke his leg.
She learned Spanish at school. She traveled to Spain.
She touched the iron. She burned her finger.
Betty baked some cookies. She ate them.
She dropped the record. She broke it.
John wrote the letter. He mailed it.
The phone rang three times. John answered it.
The light changed to red. I stopped the car.
I bought 2 tickets to the play. I asked Mary to go with me.

DRILL 57 To practice the *past perfect tense* with *after* to *emphasize* that the first action occurred *before* the second action

Note: *The* past tense *is often used in place of the* past perfect tense *by native speakers with* after, *which "carries the meaning" of sequential actions. However, the students should be familiar with the* past perfect *with* after *whenever the exact meaning is required.*

T: First, I tried on the dress.
    Then, I bought it.
S: *After I had tried on the dress, I bought it.*

First, I took out a cigarette.
Then, I lit it.

First, I picked out a book.
Then, I paid for it.

First, I made the salad.
Then, I ate it.

First, I bought the ticket.
Then, I got on the train.

First, I got the flu.
Then, I went to the doctor.

First, I turned on the TV.
Then, I watched my favorite program.

First, I got a headache.
Then, I took an aspirin.

First, I washed my hair.
Then, I dried it.

First, I studied.
Then, I took the test.

First, I fed the dog.
Then, I walked him.

DRILL 58   To practice *before* with two completed actions occurring at *two different points* of time in the past

Note: *The* past tense *is often used in place of the* past perfect tense *by native speakers with* before, *which "carries the meaning" of sequential actions. However, the students should be familiar with the past perfect and* before *whenever the exact meaning is required. If both past actions are* completed *actions, the action that occurred* first *is used in the past perfect.*

T: First, I tried on the shoes.
      Then, I bought them.
S: *I had tried on the shoes before I bought them.*

      First, I read the book.
      Then, I returned it to the library.

      First, I salted the meat.
      Then, I cooked it.

      First, I cleaned the bathtub.
      Then, I took a bath.

      First, I washed the floor.
      Then, I waxed it.

First, I cut my hair.
Then, I set it.

First, I waxed my skis.
Then, I used them.

First, I weighed the package.
Then, I put the stamps on it.

First, I took my seat.
Then, the play started.

First, I heard the record on the radio.
Then, I bought the record.

First, I read the book.
Then, I saw the movie.

First, I telephoned Mary.
Then, I visited her.

First, I saw the advertisement in the paper for the new shampoo.
Then, I bought it.

DRILL 59   To contrast *before* with the *past tense* (completed actions) and
before with the *past perfect tense* (incomplete actions)

T: I bought the coat.
      I hadn't tried it on.   (incomplete action)
S: *I bought the coat before I had tried it on.*
T: I tried on three coats.   (completed action)
      I bought this coat.
S: *I had tried on three coats before I bought this coat.*

      I took the test.
      I hadn't studied.

      I studied for three hours.
      I took the test.

      I typed the word.
      I hadn't looked it up in the dictionary.

      I looked up the word in the dictionary.
      I typed the word.

      Betty arrived at the theater.
      The play hadn't started.

      The play started.
      Betty arrived at the theater.

      We left the class.
      The bell hadn't rung.

The bell rang.
We left the class.

John took the pen.
I hadn't finished the letter.

I finished the letter.
John took the pen.

Judy wore the dress.
She hadn't paid for it.

Judy paid for the dress.
She wore it.

It started to snow.
We hadn't left the house.

We left the house.
It started to snow.

John broke the record.
He hadn't played it.

John played the record.
He broke it.

I returned the book to the library.
I hadn't read it.

I read the book.
I returned it to the library.

I saw the movie (e.g., *The Exorcist*).
I hadn't read the book.

I read the book.
I saw the movie.

DRILL 60   To practice the *past perfect tense* with *no sooner* and *just as*

T: I had just finished the cake. Then, the gas ran out.
S1: *No sooner had I finished the cake when the gas ran out.*
S2: *Just as I had finished the cake, the gas ran out.*

I had just finished the test. Then, the teacher asked for the papers.
I had just worn my new shoes. Then, the laces broke.
I had just started the letter. Then, the pen ran out of ink.
I had just balanced my checkbook. Then, I realized the total was wrong.
I had just invited John over. Then, I remembered my date with Bob.
I had just taken the car out. Then, I ran out of gas.
I had just gotten home. Then, I received your telegram.
I had just started skiing. Then, I broke my leg.
I had just locked the door. Then, I heard a knock.

I had just gotten on the train. Then, it pulled out of the station.
I had just written you a letter. Then, your letter arrived.
I had just sat down. Then, the doorbell rang.
I had just finished my homework. Then, my pen ran out of ink.
I had just hung up the telephone receiver. Then, I remembered to give her the message.

Used to express an *earlier* action that continued up to a definite *later* time in the past that is specified

DRILL 61   To practice the *past perfect tense* with *by the time . . .*

Note: *The earlier action is used with the* past perfect tense.

T: John finished the report.
     Then, he left for home.
S: *By the time John left for home, he had finished the report.*

Tom finished the test.
Then, the class ended.

The play started.
Then, John got to the theater.

Mary set the table.
Then, the guests arrived.

It started to rain.
Then, we left the house.

The store closed.
Then, Mary arrived.

The telephone stopped ringing.
Then, I got to it.

The movie started.
Then, we found our seats.

She gained 20 pounds.
Then, she started the diet.

Mary left the hospital.
Then, John decided to visit her.

The band started to play the last dance.
Then, John asked me to dance.

Mary accepted John's invitation to the party.
Then, I asked her.

It got dark outside.
Then, I left the restaurant.

DRILL 62   To practice the *past perfect tense* with *until*

Note: *The* earlier *action is used with the* past perfect tense.

T: John couldn't go to the party. First, he had to (do his homework).
S: *John couldn't go to the party until he had done his homework.*

write the letters	take a bath
eat dinner	shave
wash the dishes	wash his hair
iron his shirts	change the flat tire
call Mary	order the flowers
feed the dog	buy some wine

DRILL 63   To practice the *past perfect tense* in *dependent clauses* with statements about the past

T: John saw a new film last night.
S: *Last night John saw a film (that) he hadn't seen before.*

John visited a new museum yesterday.
Betty wore a new dress last night.
Jim read a new book last week.
George bought a new magazine yesterday.
Mary played a new card game last night.
Bill dated a new girl yesterday.
Judy saw a new play last week.
My favorite singer recorded a new song.
Judy saw a new program on TV last night.
Susan went to a new restaurant last week.
Mary cooked a new dish last night.
Betty tried a new perfume yesterday.
John smoked a new brand of cigarettes last week.
Bill learned a new dance last night.
Jim tried a new drink yesterday.

DRILL 64   To practice the *past perfect tense* in *clauses of contrast* with statements about the past

T: John saw the film a second time.
S1:   *John saw the film again, even though he had seen it before.*
S2:   *John saw the film again, although he had seen it before.*

Mary saw the play a second time.
The band played the song a second time.
The children played the game a second time.

Mary read the story a second time.
Susan visited the museum a second time.
Bill traveled to Europe a second time.
John ran the race a second time.
Judy listened to the record a second time.
Bob read the newspaper a second time.
Betty went to the concert a second time.
Susan saw the ballet a second time.

DRILL 65   To practice the *past perfect tense* in *clauses of reason* with statements about the past

A.   T: John couldn't go to the party.   (catch the flu)
      S: *John couldn't go to the party because he had caught the flu.*

buy theater tickets	make a date with Judy
have to study	have a flat tire
promise to visit his parents	take his best suit to the cleaners
break his leg	tear his pants
have an argument with Mary	leave the invitation at his office
lose the address	

B.   T: Why didn't she (take the children to the zoo)?
      S: *She didn't take the children to the zoo because she had already taken them.*

clean the room	set the alarm
see that movie	put the cat out
go to the play	feed the dog
send him a card	turn on the light
read that book	eat lunch
buy him a watch	play tennis
play that record	go to the concert
serve chicken	do her homework
pay the phone bill	take the test
open a checking account	

DRILL 66   To practice the *past perfect tense* with *reported* speech

Note: *When the verb in the direct speech is either* past *or* present perfect tense, *the* past perfect *is used for the past statement in indirect or reported speech.*

A.   T: (go to Paris)/last year
      S1:   *John went to Paris last year.*
      S2:   *Bob told us (that) John had gone to Paris last year.*

take tennis lessons	fail the test
buy a car	see Carol
paint his house	get the flu
get married	go to the hospital
study French	buy a house
travel to Spain	make a movie
lose a lot of money	sell his store
write a book	buy a boat
work in Chicago	

Note: *The following are questions to ask the students. Follow the pattern above.*

T: John, where did you go last night?
S1: *I went to the movies last night.*
S2: *John told us (that) he had gone to the movies last night.*

What did you eat for dinner last night?
What did you watch on TV last night?
What did you wear to school yesterday?
What time did you do your homework yesterday?
Who(m) did you call on the telephone last night?
What movie did you see last week?
How long did you study last night?
Where did you buy that sweater?

B. T: Were you tired last night?
    S: *He asked if I had been tired last night.*

    T: Did you go to bed early last night?
    S: *He asked if I had gone to bed early last night.*

Were you tired last night?
Did you read the newspaper yesterday?
Did you eat out last night?
Were you sick last week?
Did you take the test yesterday?
Were you angry with John last night?
Did you see the film on TV last night?
Were you bored at the lecture yesterday?
Did you finish your homework last night?
Did you buy that coat yesterday?
Were you late for school this morning?
Did you visit Mary last night?
Were you exhausted from the trip last week?
Did you read the story in the magazine last week?
Were you hungry last night?

Did you sleep well last night?
Were you happy to hear the news yesterday?
Did you enjoy the ballet last night?

C.   T: Has John eaten yet?
    S: *He asked me if John had already eaten.*

Have the children gone to bed yet?
Have they called yet?
Has Mary returned the book yet?
Has the mail arrived yet?
Has the TV program started yet?
Have they gotten the letter yet?
Has John read the book yet?
Have they seen the play yet?
Has he left for New York yet?
Have they sent the package yet?
Has he bought a new car yet?
Have they moved into the new house yet?

D.   T: What did he say?   (I didn't remember)
    S: *Last night I didn't remember what he had said, but I do now.*
    T: What did he say?   (I couldn't remember)
    S: *Last night I couldn't remember what he had said, but I can now.*

Where did he go?   (I couldn't recall)
When did he leave for Rome?   (I didn't know)
How much did he spend?   (I couldn't remember)
Where did he play tennis?   (I couldn't recall)
Who(m) did he meet?   (I didn't know)
When did he arrive at the party?   (I didn't remember)
How long did he stay?   (I couldn't say)
How many drinks did he have?   (I didn't remember)
What did he tell you?   (I couldn't recall)
How much did he eat?   (I couldn't remember)
What did he wear?   (I couldn't recall)
What did he do?   (I didn't know)
What did he bring?   (I couldn't remember)

DRILL 67   To contrast the *past perfect tense* with reported speech (direct speech in the past tense) and the *past tense* with reported speech (direct speech in the present tense)

A.   T: Does she study English every day?   (He asked . . .)
    S: *He asked if she studied English every day.*

T: Did she study English last year?
S: *He asked if she had studied English last year.*

Does she eat lunch every day?
Did she eat lunch yesterday?

Do they study every day?
Did they study yesterday?

Do they have a car?
Did they have a car last year?

Does she work at night?
Did she work at night last month?

Do they play tennis?
Did they play tennis last week?

Does he dance?
Did he dance at the party last night?

Do they play cards?
Did they play cards last week?

Does she collect stamps?
Did she collect stamps last year?

Do you watch TV every night?
Did you watch TV last night?

Do you listen to the evening news?
Did you listen to the news last night?

B.   T: Where does she work?   (He asked . . .)
S: *He asked where she worked.*

T: Where did she work last year?
S: *He asked where she had worked last year.*

How much does she eat every day?
How much did she eat for lunch?

What does she teach?
What did she teach last year?

How long does he work every day?
How long did he work yesterday?

How much does coffee cost?
How much did coffee cost last year?

Where does she live?
Where did she live last year?

What kind of cigarettes does she smoke?
What kind of cigarettes did she smoke last year?

When does the movie start?
When did the movie start last night?

How much beer does he drink?
How much beer did he drink last year?

Where does she study?
Where did she study last term?

What does he study in school?
What did he study in school last term?

C. **Note:** *When the question word is the subject of the clause in indirect speech, keep the same word order.*

    T: Who is ready?   (He asked ...)
    S: *He asked who was ready.*
    T: Who was ready an hour ago?
    S: *He asked who had been ready an hour ago.*

What is for dinner?
What was for dinner last night?

What wine is the best?
What wine was the best last year?

Which coat is on sale?
Which coat was on sale last week?

Who is here now?
Who was here yesterday?

What movie is the best this year?
What movie was the best last year?

Which car is the best this year?
Which car was the best last year?

Who is in the hospital?
Who was in the hospital last month?

Which perfume is the most expensive?
Which perfume was the most expensive last year?

DRILL 68   To contrast the *past perfect tense* with reported speech (direct speech in the *present perfect tense*) and the *past continuous tense* with reported speech (direct speech in the *present continuous tense*)

A.   T: Are you taking the children to the zoo?   (He asked ...)
        S: *He asked if I was taking the children to the zoo.*
        T: Have you taken the children to the zoo (yet)?
        S: *He asked if I had (already) taken the children to the zoo.*

Is he eating now?
Has he eaten (yet)?

Are you studying English now?
Have you studied English (yet)?

Is he watering the plants now?
Has he watered the plants (yet)?

Is he reading the newspaper now?
Has he read the newspaper (yet)?

Is he watching TV now?
Has he watched TV (yet)?

Is he listening to his records now?
Has he listened to his records (yet)?

Is he sleeping now?
Has he slept (yet)?

Is he watching the movie now?
Has he watched the movie (yet)?

Are they coming over now?
Have they come over (yet)?

Is she washing her hair now?
Has she washed her hair (yet)?

B.   T: Where is she working now?   (He asked . . .)
       S: *He asked where she was working now.*
       T: Where has she worked so far?
       S: *He asked where she had worked so far.*

What is she teaching now?
What has she taught so far?

What is she cooking now?
What has she cooked so far?

How many apples is she buying now?
How many apples has she bought so far?

What language is she studying now?
What languages has she studied so far?

Where is she traveling now?
Where has she traveled so far?

Where is the movie playing now?
Where has the movie played so far?

Where is she living now?
Where has she lived so far?

What book is he reading now?
What books has he read so far?

C. **Note:** *When the question word is the subject of the clause in indirect speech, keep the same word order.*

> T: What is happening now? (He asked . . .)
> S: *He asked what was happening now.*
> T: What has happened so far?
> S: *He asked what had happened so far.*

Who is talking now?
Who has talked so far?

Who is taking the test now?
Who has taken the test so far?

What movie is playing now?
What movies have played so far?

Who is visiting now?
Who has visited so far?

What singer is performing now?
What singers have performed so far?

Who is talking on the telephone now?
Who has talked on the telephone so far?

Who is reading now?
Who has read so far?

What football team is winning now?
What football teams have won so far?

Past Perfect Continuous Tense

To introduce the *past perfect continuous tense* to express actions in progress *up to* the time that another past action occurred

METHOD

Draw a time graph on the blackboard.

Say the following, marking the appropriate times (see graph) and placing an x for the past action. Draw solid lines to show continued past actions and vertical arrows to indicate the moment the action stopped.

T: Last night, I went to bed at 8 p.m. John called.
I had *been* sleeping for 2 hours *when* John called.
I talked to John. Then, I went back to bed. Mary called.
I had *been* sleeping for 2 hours *when* Mary called.
I talked to Mary. Then, I went back to bed. Jack called.
I had *been* sleeping for 2 hours *when* Jack called.
I talked to Jack. Then, I went back to bed. The alarm went off.
I had *been* sleeping for 6 hours *when* the alarm went off.

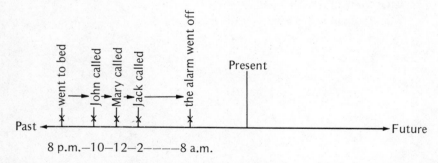

8 p.m.—10—12—2————8 a.m.

Note: *The continuous past action* stopped *when the past action occurred, in contrast to the use of* when *with the* past continuous tense, *where the action still continues.*

REPEAT

Activity 1: Make a new time graph.
Ask the students: "How long had you been sleeping when your alarm went off this morning?"
Mark on the time graph as above.

Activity 2: Make a new time graph.

Ask the students: "How long had you been studying English in (your country) when you came to the United States?"

Mark on the time graph as above.

Used to emphasize the duration of time and the continuity of action (more so than the *past perfect tense*) for an action which began in the past and continues to the time that another past action occurred

DRILL 69   To practice the *past perfect continuous tense* with *when* and the past tense

A.   T: He has been waiting for 3 hours.   (train pull in)
        S: *He had been waiting for 3 hours when the train pulled in.*

John has been working all day.   (the boss/comes over)
Jack has been cooking all afternoon.   (run out of gas)
Bill has been calling the waiter for 10 minutes.   (come over)
I have been dancing for 2 hours.   (John/arrive)
They have been playing football for 3 hours.   (rain/start)
Linda has been knitting all morning.   (run out of yarn)
He has been skiing all afternoon.   (break his leg)
They have been standing all morning.   (the bus/come)
We have been listening to music for 3 hours.   (news/come on)
He has been eating breakfast for an hour.   (mailman/come)
They have been waiting in line for an hour.   (clerk/come)
John has been studying all evening.   (the telephone/ring)

B.   T: He was sleeping for 8 hours.
            Then, he got up.
        S: *He had been sleeping for 8 hours when he got up.*

He was watching TV for 3 hours.
Then, he turned it off.

He was listening to music on the radio for an hour.
Then, he heard the news.

He was studying for 4 hours.
Then, he went to bed.

He was shopping for 5 hours.
Then, he stopped for coffee.

He was typing for 6 hours.
Then, he changed the ribbon.

He was cleaning the house for 4 hours.
Then, the doorbell rang.

He was cooking for 3 hours.
Then, the guests arrived.

He was doing his homework for 8 hours.
Then, Mary came over.

He was fixing the car for 4 hours.
Then, he found the problem.

He was fishing for 5 hours.
Then, he caught a fish.

C.   T: John watched the movie for 20 minutes.
             Then he realized that he had seen it last year.
      S: *John had been watching the movie for 20 minutes when he*
           realized that he had seen it before.

He read the book for an hour.
Then, he realized that he had read it last year.

He ironed the shirt for 5 minutes.
Then, he realized that he had ironed it last week.

He did the homework for a half hour.
Then, he realized that he had done it last week.

He watched the TV program for 15 minutes.
Then, he realized that he had seen it last month.

He listened to the tape for 10 minutes.
Then, he realized that he had heard it last week.

He typed the report for 15 minutes.
Then, he realized that he had typed it last week.

He looked through the magazine for 10 minutes.
Then, he realized that he had read it last month.

He skied the trail for 15 minutes.
Then, he realized that he had skied it last winter.

He drove on the highway for a half hour.
Then, he realized that he had taken it last summer.

He ate the special dessert for 5 minutes.
Then, he realized that he had tried it last year.

DRILL 70   To practice the special use of the *past perfect continuous tense*
with *want to*

T: I finally saw that movie.

S: *I had been wanting to see that movie for a long time (before I finally saw it).*

I finally read that book.
John finally got a Mercedes sports car.
Mary finally got married.
My son finally got a dog.
My parents finally went to Europe.
I finally went to graduate school.
John finally bought a summer house.
Bill finally got a good job.
Judy finally bought a fur coat.
Mr. Smith finally took a vacation.
Bob finally bought a stereo.
Tim finally went to Las Vegas.

DRILL 71 To practice the *past perfect continuous tense* with *after* to emphasize the *recency* and *duration* of the previous action in the past

T: I studied all evening.
Then, I finally went to bed.

S: *After I had been studying all evening, I finally went to bed.*

Bob drove 250 miles.
Then, he finally reached home.

The secretary typed all morning.
Then, she finally went for coffee.

John looked for the book for hours.
Then, he finally found it.

Bob typed for hours.
Then, he finally took a break.

Susan lived with her parents for years.
Then, she finally got her own apartment.

Mary wore her hair long for years.
Then, she finally got it cut.

Judy waited in line for the tickets for 3 hours.
Then, she couldn't find her checkbook.

Betty stood at the bus stop for an hour.
Then, she couldn't find a seat on the bus.

Bob tried to call Paris for hours.
Then, he finally got the overseas operator.

Mary sat in the waiting room for 2 hours.
Then, she finally saw the doctor.

Bob studied at the university for 6 years.
Then, he finally got his degree.

Mary lived in Europe for 10 years.
Then, she finally moved back to the States.

DRILL 72 To practice the *past perfect continuous tense* with *before* to emphasize the recency and duration of the previous *completed* past action

Note: *The action that occurred* first *is used in the* past perfect continuous tense.

T: Mary tried on dresses all afternoon.
     Then, she finally bought one.
S: *Mary had been trying on dresses all afternoon before she (finally) bought one.*

Susan went out with John for 3 years.
Then, she finally married him.

Judy looked at the menu for 20 minutes.
Then, she finally ordered.

John danced with the girl for 10 minutes.
Then, he finally asked her name.

Jim wore glasses for 10 years.
Then, he finally bought contact lenses.

Bill complained about a toothache for months.
Then, he finally went to the dentist.

Judy waited for John's letter for 2 weeks.
Then, it finally arrived.

Bill carried his camera all afternoon.
Then, he finally took a photograph.

Tim studied for the exam for 2 years.
Then, he finally passed it.

John tried to get a taxi for a half hour.
Then, he finally got one.

Betty waited at the subway station for 40 minutes.
Then, her train finally came.

John gained 10 pounds every year.
Then, he finally went on a diet.

Judy worked 10 hours a day for the past 3 years.
Then, she finally took a long vacation.

DRILL 73   To practice the *past perfect continuous tense* with *because*

A.   T: John worked hard all afternoon.
                He took a nap.
         S: *John took a nap because he had been working hard all afternoon.*

   John studied all day.
   He got an A on the test.

   Mary's old car gave her trouble all the time.
   She bought a new car.

   Bob trained 4 hours a day for a year.
   He won the big race.

   Susan worked hard all year.
   She took a long vacation.

   Mary shopped all morning.
   She stopped for a rest.

   Bill drank beer all evening.
   He had a headache.

   Bill played tennis all afternoon.
   He took a hot bath.

   Bob listened to the record all afternoon.
   He knew the words of the song.

   Bill worked on the car all morning.
   He changed his clothes.

   Judy worked in the garden all afternoon.
   She had a backache.

B.   T: Why was she tired?   (work all afternoon)
         S: *Because she had been working all afternoon.*

   Why did she get wet?   (walk in the rain)
   Why were they late?   (talk on the telephone)
   Why were you ill?   (not take medicine)
   Why did you bring your racquet?   (play tennis/all afternoon)
   Why was she wearing an apron?   (cook/all afternoon)
   Why were her eyes red?   (cry/all night)
   Why did you wear your old clothes?   (fix the car)
   Why were you nervous?   (study for the test)
   Why did you have ink on your hands?   (type letters/all day)
   Why did she have flour on her shirt?   (bake/all morning)
   Why were you tired?   (travel/all night)
   Why did your feet ache?   (stand/all afternoon)
   Why was she angry?   (wait for me/all night)
   Why were you late?   (wait for a bus)

Why did she have a backache?   (lift boxes/all morning)
Why did he bring a football?   (play football/all day)
Why were you upset?   (wait for an important telegram)
Why did you take another shower?   (work on the car/all day)

DRILL 74   To practice the *past perfect continuous tense* with reported speech

T: Have you been sitting for a long time?   (He asked . . .)
S: *He asked if I had been sitting for a long time.*
T: Where have you been eating your lunch lately?
S: *He asked where I had been eating my lunch lately.*

Has she been working long hours lately?
What has he been doing this long?
Have they been shopping all this time?
What books have you been using in school this term?
What kind of car has he been driving this year?
Have they been living in (New York) all this time?
What classes has he been teaching this term?
Has she been typing all morning?
How long has he been wearing those shoes?
Has he been drinking all night?
Where has he been living all these years?
Have they been traveling a lot recently?

Future Simple Tense

To introduce actions expected to occur after the moment of speaking

METHOD
>   Draw a time graph on the blackboard.
>   Say the following, marking an x to indicate future action.

T: I see you every day. I am going to see ← you tomorrow.
                      will see   the day after tomorrow
                      am seeing   next week
                                           next month
                                           next year

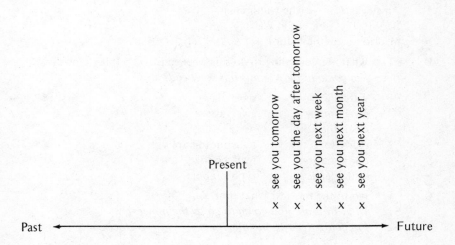

REPEAT

Activity: Make a new time graph.
              Ask the students: "What are you going to do tonight?
                              will you do
                              are you doing
                      tomorrow? next week? etc.

Used to express expected or intended action from the moment of speaking

DRILL 75   To practice *going to* to express future action

A.   T: When are you going to go to   (London)?
       S1:   *I'm going to go to London tomorrow.*
       T: (see)
       S2:   *What are you going to see in London?*
       S3:   *I'm going to see (Big Ben) in London.*

Paris   (the Eiffel Tower)
New York   (the Empire State Building)
Moscow   (the Kremlin)
Athens   (the Parthenon)
Rome   (the Colosseum)
Cairo   (the Pyramids)
California   (Disneyland)
Amsterdam   (the windmills)
Berlin   (the Berlin Wall)
Madrid   (the Prado)

B.   T: What are you going to do this weekend?   (play tennis)
       S: *I'm going to play tennis this weekend?*

watch TV   see a play
go shopping   give a party
clean the house   write letters
study for a test   take photographs
do homework   read a book
visit friends   type a report

C.   T: (go to the movies) What time . . .
       S1:   *What time are you going to go to the movies?*
       S2:   *I'm going to go to the movies at _____ o'clock.*

watch that TV program   meet me
do your homework   go for coffee
cook dinner   go to the hospital
walk to the library   go to bed
take the bus   get up tomorrow
call me tonight   go to work
come over

D.   T: Mary is taking out the sewing machine.   (make a dress)
       S: *Mary is going to make a dress.*

Bill is buying a novel.   (read a book)
Judy is setting up the ironing board.   (press her clothes)

Bob is looking for a parking space.   (park his car)
Betty is putting some film in her camera.   (take some photographs)
Jim is sharpening the saw.   (cut some wood)
Michael is turning the TV on.   (watch the news)
Tim is taking out the typewriter.   (type a report)
Judy is looking through the cookbook.   (try a new recipe)
Bob is putting up the card table.   (play cards)
Greg is opening the letter.   (read the letter)
John is getting the dictionary.   (look up a word)
Tom is opening a bottle of wine.   (drink some wine)
The students are taking all books and papers off their desks.   (take
  a test)

E.   T: Whose party are you going to go to?
        S: *I'm going to go to Mary's party.*

Where is the party going to be?
When is the party going to start?
What are you going to wear to the party?
Who's going to go to the party?
How long is the party going to last?
How many people are going to go to the party?
What time is the party going to end?
How many bottles of wine are you going to bring to the party?
What gift are you going to give Mary?
What are you going to do after the party?
How are you going to get to the party?
How are you going to get home from the party?

F.   T: What are you going to (eat for dinner)?
      S1:   *I'm going to eat _____ for dinner.*
    S1 to
      S2:   *What are you going to eat for dinner?*
      S2:   *I'm going to eat _____ for dinner.*
          etc.

wear to school tomorrow	get for your birthday
do on your vacation	buy at the store
watch on TV tonight	see at the theater
see at the movies this week	cook for lunch tomorrow
listen to on the radio	do on Saturday night
get for Christmas	buy at the pet store

G.   T: John is learning to fly airplanes.   (pilot)
        S: *He's going to be a pilot.*

cook   (chef)
drive a taxi   (taxi driver)

make drinks	(bartender)
teach English	(English teacher)
take dictation	(secretary)
direct traffic	(policeman)
put out fires	(fireman)
bake bread	(baker)
fix cars	(mechanic)
repair pipes	(plumber)
sell cars	(car salesman)
cut hair	(hairdresser)
raise chickens	(chicken farmer)
drive a bus	(bus driver)
run a computer	(computer programmer)
cut meat	(butcher)
collect garbage	(garbage collector)
catalog books	(librarian)

H. T: John plans to give a party. (invite 50 people)
    S: *He's going to invite 50 people.*

Mary plans to take a trip. (go to London)
The children plan to visit the zoo. (see the elephants)
Jim plans to study medicine. (become a doctor)
Judy plans to study. (take a test)
Arthur plans to fix his car. (change the oil)
They plan to spend the night. (use the guest room)
The girls plan to meet us later. (wait at the library)
Jane plans to study law. (become a lawyer)
Jack plans to cook lunch. (serve hamburgers)
I plan to go on a business trip. (take the train)
We plan to see you later. (come over tonight)
Betty plans to bring the dessert. (make some brownies)
John plans to go to the university. (study biology)
Susan plans to enter the talent contest. (sing a song)
Bob plans to read a book. (read *Gone With the Wind*)
The students plan to take a field trip. (visit the museum)

DRILL 76 To practice *going to* to express *certainty* about a future event or action

A. T: I studied for 10 hours. (pass the test)
    S: *(I'm sure) I'm going to pass the test.*

I got an invitation to the party and I bought a new dress. (go to the party)
I practiced my new serve for 2 weeks. (win the tennis match)

I didn't eat breakfast.   (eat a big lunch)
I borrowed $10 from John.   (pay him back)
I watched Part I of the movie last night. Part II is on tonight.
    (watch Part II)
I walked in the rain without an umbrella.   (get a cold)
I made reservations at a very expensive restaurant.   (spend a lot of
    money)
I didn't write the composition.   (stay home tonight)
I borrowed a book from John.   (return it soon)
I found a good job.   (make a lot of money)

B.   T: Black clouds are moving in.   (rain)
         S: *It's going to rain.*

I didn't study for the test.   (fail)
He's driving too fast.   (have an accident)
He's a bad skier.   (break his leg)
John's overeating.   (get sick)
He doesn't know she's married.   (get angry)
His horse lost the race.   (lose his money)
His books are overdue.   (pay a fine)
Her car broke down.   (spend a lot of money)
The flight is canceled.   (wait for the next one)
There are no more seats.   (stand up)
We have to leave early.   (miss the ending)
It's really cold today.   (get a cold)
The boat is full of water.   (sink)
The car is parked on the wrong side of the street.   (get a ticket)
John's drinking too much.   (get drunk)
Mary is lifting a lot of boxes.   (get a backache)
The children are playing in the mud.   (get dirty)
The policeman caught the thief.   (go to jail)

DRILL 77   To practice *going to* to express *refusal*

T: I took 3 tests today.
S: *I'm not going to take that test (today)!*

I cleaned my room this morning.
I cooked dinner every night last week.
I took out the garbage yesterday.
I stayed home and studied every night last week.
I listened to that boring teacher every day last term.
I had them over twice last week.
I rewrote that composition twice.
I visited my aunt three times last week.

I waited 3 hours for the appointment last month.
I washed the dishes last night.
I saw that movie three times.
I fixed the stereo twice last week.
I watched that TV movie three times last year.
I ate chicken three times last week.
I read that book twice last year.

DRILL 78   To practice *going to* with *before* and *after* and the present tense

T: (do his homework)
S: *John is going to do his homework before he goes to bed.*

clean his room	write some letters
call Mary	read a book
write the composition	visit his friends
watch TV	water the plants
shine his shoes	wash his hair
type a report	take a bath

Note: *Have the students ask each other:*

What are you going to do before you go to bed?
What are you going to do before you leave school today?
What are you going to do before this weekend?
What are you going to see before you leave (New York)?

Repeat (do his homework) for: John is going to go to bed after he does his homework.

Have the students ask each other:

What are you going to do after this class (finishes)?
What are you going to do after you graduate from school?
What are you going to do after you eat dinner tonight?

DRILL 79   To practice *will* to express future action

A.   T: Did you (clean your room)?
          S: *No, I'll clean it tomorrow.*

wash your hair	look for the pen
do the dishes	wash the floor
write the letter	fix the clock
study for the test	wax the car
read the newspaper	see the movie
send the package	listen to the record
call her back	watch that TV program
return the books	write the composition

B.   T: (go to the museum)
    S1:   *Are you going to go to the museum?*
    S2:   *I'm going to, but John isn't. He's going to go to _____ .*
    S3:   *Will you go to the museum?*
    S4:   *I will, but John won't. He'll go to _____ .*

play football	go on a trip
travel to Spain	take a vacation
take the train	see a film
practice the piano	read a book
ride the bicycle	listen to records
take the plane	cook dinner
go shopping	study for the test
buy a new car	visit Mary

DRILL 80   To practice *will* to express *promise*

A.   T: I promise to (do it soon).
    S: *Yes, I will. I'll do it soon.*

take care of it	take care of the children
send the letter	read that book
take the notes	answer the letter
clean my room	call you tomorrow
drive slowly	visit you soon
be careful	take care of your plants
see you soon	

B.   T: I promise not to (smoke again).
    S: *I won't smoke again.*

tell your secret	bother you
cheat on the test	waste your time
give out your telephone number	drink too much
make that mistake again	drive so fast
write in pencil	eat so much
leave the room	talk so much

DRILL 81   To practice *won't* to express *refusal*

A.   T: John refuses to (come with us).
    S: *John won't come with us.*

invite her	wear a tie
clean his room	press his suit
do his homework	cook dinner
get his license	take her out

wash his hair   dance
eat spinach   see that play
shine his shoes   go to the ballet
pay the bill

B.   T: The cover is stuck on the jar.   (come off)
     S: *It won't come off.*

This stain is tough.   (wipe off)
The nail is stuck.   (come out)
This pen is out of ink.   (write)
This radio is broken.   (play)
This alarm clock is broken.   (go off)
This needle is rusty.   (sew)
My hair is straight.   (curl)
My ring is stuck.   (come off)
The iron is broken.   (get hot)
The cork is stuck.   (come out)
My pants are big.   (stay up)
My shoes are big.   (stay on)

DRILL 82   To practice *will* to express *volunteered* actions

T: I forgot my coat.   (lend)
S: *I'll lend you mine.*

I forgot my pen.   (lend)
I need a ride.   (take)
I ripped my shirt.   (sew)
I haven't eaten dinner.   (cook)
I don't want to go alone.   (walk)
I need a button for my shirt.   (give)
I have to move the piano.   (help)
Mr. Smith's not in today.   (call back later)
The baby's crying.   (change)
The children are hungry.   (feed)
The dog wants to go out.   (walk)
John needs company.   (talk)
Mary is in the hospital.   (visit)
The plants need water.   (water)

DRILL 83   To practice short answers with *will* and *going to*

T: Will he stay? No . . .
S: *No, he won't.*

T: Will he come later? Yes . . .
S: *Yes, he will.*
T: Is he going to call? No . . .
S: *No, he isn't.*
T: Is he going to study later? Yes . . .
S: *Yes, he is.*

Will he write soon? No . . .
Is she going to come? No . . .
Are they going to meet us? Yes . . .
Will she get the tickets? No . . .
Are we going to eat later? Yes . . .
Are they going to take a vacation? No . . .
Will he wait? No . . .
Is she going to call? Yes . . .
Will you join us? Yes . . .
Are we going to see a film? No . . .
Will she visit us soon? Yes . . .
Will they take the test soon? No . . .
Is he going to go skiing? No . . .
Are you going to call? Yes . . .
Will they go shopping? No . . .
Will it snow tomorrow? Yes . . .
Is he going to see the movie? No . . .
Will she go skiing tomorrow? Yes . . .
Are we going to see the play? No . . .
Will it rain tonight? Yes . . .

DRILL 84   To practice *shall* to express future action

Note: Shall *is rarely used in everyday conversation. Most often it is used in polite forms like "suggestions."*

T: Let's (have a party).
S: *Shall we have a party?*

eat now	make reservations
go for a drink	send them a postcard
serve the dessert	go out for dinner
play cards now	send them a wedding gift
have them over	play the new records
go over the guest list	visit the museum

Note: *See the* present continuous tense, *used to express future action.*

Future Continuous Tense

To introduce actions taking place *at* or *up to* a definite time in the future

METHOD

Draw a time graph on the blackboard; indicate the class period (see graph).

Say the following, marking an x to indicate future action; draw a line across the x, to show continuous future activity.

T: Right now, I am talking to you. Tomorrow, from 11 to 2 (class time), I will be talking to you.

Right now, I am standing in front of the class. Tomorrow, from 11 to 2, I will be standing in front of you.

Right now, I am teaching a lesson. Tomorrow, from 11 to 2, I will be teaching a lesson.

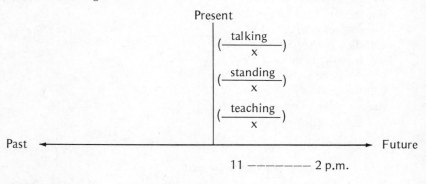

REPEAT

Activity 1: Make a new time graph.

Ask the students: "What are you doing right now? What will you be doing this time tomorrow?"

Mark on the time graph as above.

Activity 2: Make a new time graph.

Ask the students: "What will you be doing from 2 to 4 (4 to 6, 6 to 8, 8 to 10, 10 to 12, etc.) tomorrow?"

Mark on the time graph as above.

Used to express an action that is taking place *at* or *up to* a definite time in the future

DRILL 85   To contrast the *future continuous tense* with the *present continuous tense*

A.   T: I'm studying English now.   (French)
    S1:   *This time tomorrow, I'll be studying French.*
    S2:   *This time tomorrow, I'm going to be studying French.*

I'm writing a story now.   (book)
I'm eating a steak.   (fish)
I'm waiting for Jack.   (Bill)
I'm playing football.   (tennis)
I'm seeing a movie.   (play)
I'm talking to John.   (Betty)
I'm visiting Judy.   (Susan)
I'm walking to the library.   (museum)
I'm traveling to New York.   (Chicago)
I'm taking the bus.   (train)
I'm listening to the radio.   (records)
I'm sitting in the living room.   (den)
I'm doing homework.   (dishes)
I'm going to school.   (hospital)

B.   T: This year, I'm (studying in New York).   (Chicago)
    S1:   *Next year, I'll be studying in Chicago.*
    S2:   *Next year, I'm going to be studying in Chicago.*

working in law   (business)
living in Los Angeles   (Washington)
traveling in Africa   (Asia)
driving a Ford   (Volkswagen)
buying a 3-bedroom house   (5-bedroom house)
eating hamburgers   (steak)
wearing blue jeans   (suits)
buying a black and white TV   (color)
taking the train   (plane)
writing short stories   (novel)

DRILL 86   To practice the *future continuous tense* with *definite* times in the future

A.   T: Mary hasn't finished (the test) yet.   (write)
    S: *She'll be writing for another hour.*

the dinner   (cook)   the portrait   (paint)
the dress   (sew)   the book   (read)
the sweater   (knit)   the clothes   (wash)

the housework   (clean)   the shirts   (iron)
the report   (type)   the composition   (write)
the movie   (watch)

B.   T: John is going to come for the letter.   (write the letter)
        S: *I'll be writing the letter when John arrives.*

John is going to come for dinner.   (cook the dinner)
John is going to come for the skis.   (wax the skis)
John is going to come for the book.   (read the last chapter)
John is going to come for the shirt.   (iron the shirt)
John is going to come for the photographs.   (develop the prints)
John is going to come for the cake.   (put on the frosting)
John is going to come for the shoes.   (shine the shoes)
John is going to come for the silver.   (polish the silver)
John is going to come for the night.   (clean the guest room)
John is going to come for the car.   (wash the car)
John is going to come for the children.   (dress the children)
John is going to come for the report.   (type the last chapter)

C.   T: I have a dinner reservation at 8 o'clock.   (eat dinner)
        S: *I'll be eating dinner at 8 o'clock.*

I have a doctor's appointment at 5 o'clock.   (get a physical examination)
I have a dentist's appointment at 4 o'clock.   (get my teeth cleaned)
I have a hairdresser's appointment at 2 o'clock.   (get a haircut)
I have a luncheon engagement at 1 o'clock.   (have lunch)
I have a dinner party to attend at 7 o'clock.   (eat dinner)
I have a job interview at 10 o'clock.   (apply for a job)
I have a dress fitting at 3 o'clock.   (try on my dress)
I have a staff meeting at 11 o'clock.   (give a report)
I have a court case at 9 o'clock.   (defend my client)
I have a cocktail party to attend at 6 o'clock.   (have drinks)
I have a committee meeting at 4 o'clock.   (listen to a report)
I have a class at 2 o'clock.   (take notes)
I have an examination at 3 o'clock.   (take a test)

DRILL 87   To practice the *future continuous tense* with *because*

T: I won't be able to go to the party.   (travel in Europe)
S1:   *I won't be able to go to the party because I'll be traveling in Europe then.*
S2:   *I won't be able to go to the party because I'm going to be traveling in Europe then.*

We won't be able to have the picnic.   (rain/tomorrow)
John won't be able to come.   (visit/his parents)
Mary won't be able to see the movie.   (watch TV)
Judy won't be able to use the car.   (take the train)
John won't be able to answer the phone.   (take a bath)
John won't be able to be in class.   (take a test)
Judy won't be able to come.   (clean the house)
Jane won't be able to cook.   (do the shopping)
Jack won't be able to play golf.   (play tennis)
The children won't be able to come.   (go to school)
Bill won't be able to pick us up.   (work late)
Carl won't be able to have dinner with us.   (type the report)

DRILL 88   To practice the *future continuous tense* with a *second* future action

T: First, eat salad.
       Then, eat steak.
S1:   *First, we'll eat salad; then, we'll be eating steak.*
S2:   *First, we're going to eat salad; then, we're going to be eating steak.*

First, see Big Ben.
Then, see the British Museum.

First, visit my parents.
Then, visit your parents.

First, study English.
Then, study history.

First, open the cards.
Then, open the presents.

First, see the cartoons.
Then, see the film.

First, get engaged.
Then, get married.

First, buy the house.
Then, buy the furniture.

First, get a license.
Then, buy a car.

First, write a letter.
Then, send it.

First, serve dinner.
Then, serve dessert and coffee.

First, write a report.
Then, type it.
First, get a hotel.
Then, go for a walk.

DRILL 89 To practice the special use of the *future continuous tense* with expected events

A. T: John's car is out of gas. (drive)
S1: *John won't be driving the car.*
S2: *John isn't going to be driving the car.*

Jim's radio is broken. (listen to music)
Mary's stove is out of order. (cook)
I don't have any cigarettes. (smoke)
John's car has a flat tire. (drive)
There's no more food in our house. (eat)
Our lights aren't working. (read)
Mary's baby is crying. (sleep)
John lost all his money. (play cards)
John's whisky is all gone. (drink)
Our phone is out of order. (get calls)
Jim's racket is broken. (play tennis)
Our hot-water tank is broken. (take a shower)
Jack failed the test. (graduate)
Judy lost her wallet. (buy a new dress)
Bob gained 10 pounds. (eat dessert)
Susan lost her library card. (take out books)
Larry ran out of stamps. (mail letters)
Judy's typewriter is broken. (type the report)
Betty's out of yarn. (knit)
I left my books in school. (do homework)

B. T: John finished school last year. (study English)
S1: *He won't be studying English any more.*
S2: *He isn't going to be studying English any more.*

do homework	take quizzes
write exercises	sit in class
take tests	ask questions in class
type papers	go to language laboratories
give reports	buy textbooks
study tenses	take notes
do drills	

C.   T: John got married today.   (cook)
       S1: *He won't be cooking any more.*
       S2: *He isn't going to be cooking any more.*

iron his shirts	drink beer every night
clean the house	meet girls
wash his clothes	buy a lot of clothes
make his breakfast	get drunk
stay out late	drive a sports car
make dates	eat frozen dinners
play cards with the boys	

Future Perfect Tense

To introduce an action that will be completed or will occur before a definite time in the future

METHOD

Draw a time graph on the blackboard; indicate Friday (see graph).
Say the following, marking the future action.

T: I am teaching the unit.
            correcting your papers.
            writing a test.
            reviewing the verbs.
      By Friday, I will have finished teaching the unit.
                            correcting your papers.
                            writing a test.
                            reviewing the verbs.

REPEAT

Activity: Make a new time graph; indicate 12 midnight instead of Friday.
              Ask the students: "What are you going to do today? By 12 midnight, you will have _____ ."
              Mark on the time graph as above.

Used to express an action that will be completed or will occur before a definite time in the future

DRILL 90   To introduce the *future perfect tense*

A.   T: Can I have the book on Friday?   (finish)
          S: *I'll have finished it by then.*

Can I have the dress on Friday? (wear)
Can I have the record on Tuesday? (listen to)
Can I have the radio on Wednesday? (fix)
Can I have the magazine on Tuesday? (read)
Can I have the slides on Sunday? (see)
Can I have the iron on Thursday? (use)
Can I have the tennis racket on Saturday? (play tennis)
Can I have the money on Friday? (save)
Can I have the blouse on Monday? (wash)
Can I have the suit on Wednesday? (press)
Can I have the typewriter on Sunday? (finish the report)
Can I have the camera on Thursday? (take the photographs)

B.   T: Will you decide by Tuesday? (make up your mind)
   S: *Yes, I will have made up my mind by then.*

   T: Can you meet us after work? (leave)
   S: *No, I will have left by then.*

Will you stay here for the summer? (go to London)
Will you study here next year? (graduate)
Can you be ready at 6 o'clock? (finish my homework)
Will you watch the 12 o'clock movie? (go to bed)
Can you have dinner with us at 9 o'clock? (eat)
Will you need my typewriter next week? (buy one)
Will you send the report tomorrow? (write it)
Can you return my library books next week? (go there)
Will you go with me to see that new movie next week? (see it)
Can I help you bake the cookies tonight? (made them)

C.   T: The watch is broken. (fix)
   S: *We'll have had it fixed by Saturday.*

The stereo is out of order. (repair)
The shoes need a shine. (shine)
The clothes are dirty. (wash)
The walls need painting. (paint)
Your homework isn't finished. (do)
We need shelves in the kitchen. (build)
The tire is flat. (change)
The floor needs waxing. (polish)
The tub is dirty. (clean)
The pipes are leaking. (fix)
The report isn't typed. (type)
The floors need washing. (wash)

D.   T: Have you (seen that movie) yet?
   S1:   *Not yet, but I will have seen it by Saturday.*
   S2:   *Not yet, but I will have seen it before Saturday.*

written that letter	seen the principal
cleaned your room	entered the contest
bought a car	mailed the package
painted the house	taken the new train
returned the book	cashed your paycheck
fixed the TV	written the report
had a blood test	washed the car
gotten the flu shot	seen that new play

E.   Questions to ask the students:

What will have happened to you by this time tomorrow?
                                                next week?
                                                next month?
                                                next year?

What will have happened by the year 2000?
   What about war?
                    peace?
                    cancer?
                    poverty?
                    population growth?
                    life on Mars?
                    space travel?
                    pollution?
                    food?
                    energy supplies?
                    computers?
                    nuclear energy?

DRILL 91   To practice the *future perfect tense* when making assumptions
about the present

T: Let's call John now.   (leave)
S: *He will have left by now.*

Let's see the movie now.   (start)
Let's go to the sale now.   (finish)
Let's meet the plane now.   (arrive)
Let's call Mary now.   (go to bed)
Let's tell Betty now.   (hear)

Let's invite John to lunch now.   (eat)
Let's meet Bob after work.   (go home)
Let's watch that TV program now.   (end)
Let's visit Margaret now.   (go out)
Let's go to the hospital and see Judy.   (recover)
Let's sell the car to Mary.   (buy one)
Let's go to the store.   (close)

Future Perfect Continuous Tense

To introduce continuous actions that will have been taking place up to a definite point in the future

METHOD

    Draw a time graph on the blackboard.

    Say the following, marking the present perfect continuous aspect with a line of x's from the start of the action up to the definite point (June).

T: I have been teaching this class   for 3 months.
                 correcting your homework
                 writing tests
                 grading compositions
    By June, I will have been (teaching this class) for 8 months.

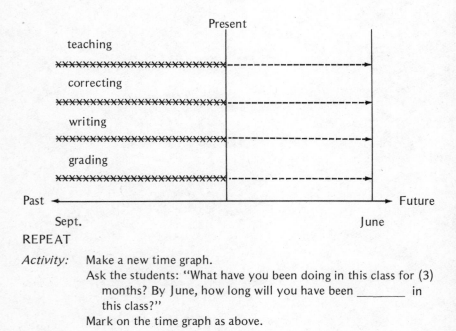

REPEAT

Activity: Make a new time graph.
           Ask the students: "What have you been doing in this class for (3) months? By June, how long will you have been _____ in this class?"
           Mark on the time graph as above.

Used to emphasize an action that *has been occurring* up to some other definite point in the future

DRILL 92   To introduce the *future perfect continuous tense*

A.   T: We've been (living in New York for 3 years). By next year . . .
     S: *By next year, we will have been living in New York for 4 years.*

studying English for 2 years   (By next year . . .)
taking the bus for 8 years
traveling in Europe for 4 years
working in this office for 10 years
living in this house for 20 years
drinking coke for 12 years
watching this TV program for 3 years
writing this book for 6 years
seeing this doctor for 9 years
taking tennis lessons for 5 years
playing golf for 7 years
going to that resort for 15 years
shopping at this store for 8 years

B.   T: She's marrying him in August.   (dating/3 months)
     S: *She will have been dating him for 3 months.*

John's taking the exam in September.   (study/6 weeks)
Judy's making a dress for tonight.   (sew/8 hours)
John's attending a meeting.   (sit/4 hours)
Mr. Smith's giving a lecture.   (talk/3 hours)
Jack's driving to Boston.   (travel/6 hours)
John's retiring in June.   (work/40 years)
Mary's reviewing a book.   (read/16 hours)
Jim's working on his master's degree.   (study/3 years)
Judy's shopping for a new dress.   (look at clothes/6 hours)
Jim's giving a concert.   (practice/6 months)
Betty's working in the kitchen.   (cook/3 hours)
John's preparing for the football game.   (practice/5 hours)
Bob's calling all his friends on the telephone.   (talk/4 hours)
Betty's working in the garden.   (dig/2 hours)

Conditionals

	Condition	Result
First conditional	*Present real situation* If it rains, 　(V)	*present* I wear a raincoat.
	If John asks me to go to the party, 　(V)	*future* I'll go.
	If the phone rings, 　(V)	*imperative* answer it.
Second conditional	*Present unreal situation* If the phone were ringing now, 　(were + V-ing) If the phone rang, 　(v-ed)	I would answer it. 　(would + V-stem) I would answer it. 　(would + V-stem)
Third conditional	*Past unreal situation* If John had asked me to the party, 　(had + V-ed, en)	I would have gone. 　(would + have + V-ed, en)

Used to express a real or unreal situation that is expected as a result of some specified condition or requirement

The First Conditional: present real
Used when the condition is *possible* and the result refers to a *present* or *future* situation
　　condition—present tense
　　result—present or future tense; imperative

DRILL 93　　To practice the *first conditional* with commands

T:　The phone might ring. Answer it.
S:　*If the phone rings, answer it.*

　　The dog might bark. Take him out.
　　The baby might cry. Feed him.
　　The mail might come_ Open it.
　　You might see John. Give him the message.
　　The TV might be too loud. Turn it down.
　　The gas man might come. Pay him.

John might come over. Give him coffee.
The light might go off. Change the bulb.
It might rain. Take your umbrella.
Mr. Smith might call. Take the message.
The package might arrive. Open it.
Judy might call. Tell her the news.

DRILL 94   To practice the *first conditional* with general truths

T: What happens if you use a credit card to buy a dress?
S: *If I use a credit card to buy a dress, I (get the bill a month later).*

What happens if you wear shoes that are too small for you?
What happens if you fail an English test?
What happens if you miss the bus to school?
What happens if you return a library book late?
What happens if your alarm clock goes off?
What happens if you don't water your plants?
What happens if you don't pay your telephone bill?
What happens if you don't do your homework?
What happens if you get sick?
What happens if you get a headache?
What happens if you don't put milk in the refrigerator?
What happens if you don't wash your clothes?
What happens if you don't eat?
What happens if you don't shave every day?

DRILL 95   To practice the *first conditional* with future results

A.   T: I might visit Mary. I'll tell her about the party.
     S: *If I visit Mary, I'll tell her about the party.*

I might go to the theater. I'll take a taxi.
I might come late. I'll sit in the back.
I might go to the party. I'll bring the wine.
I might finish the book. I'll give it to you.
I might write the letter. I'll mail it tonight.
I might cook dinner. I'll invite you over.
I might buy a new dress. I'll wear it tomorrow.
I might cash a check. I'll give you the money.
I might go to Chicago. I'll take the 2 o'clock train.
I might borrow a book. I'll return it tomorrow.

B.   T: I think John is coming.
I want to tell him the news.
S: *If John comes, I'll tell him the news.*

I think Judy is calling.
I want to talk to her.

I think it's going to rain.
I need to use an umbrella.

I think I'm getting sick.
I need to take my medicine.

I think I'm going to Mexico.
I want to buy a new camera.

I think I'm gaining weight.
I need to go on a diet.

I think I'm getting a toothache.
I need to go to the dentist.

I think John is driving to New York.
I want to go with him.

I think I'm seeing John.
I want to invite him to the party.

I think it's getting sunny.
I want to have a picnic.

I think I'm going to the party.
I want to wear my new dress.

C.   T: I want to buy a new car. I'll buy a (favorite car).
S: *If I buy a new car, I'll buy a Ford.*

I want to take a trip. I'll go to (favorite place).
I want to see a play. I'll see (favorite play)
I want to get a new pet. I'll get a (favorite pet).
I want to eat out. I'll go to (favorite restaurant).
I want to read a book. I'll read (favorite book).
I want to buy a magazine. I'll buy (favorite magazine).
I want to have a drink. I'll drink (favorite drink).
I want to see a movie. I'll see (favorite movie).
I want to study a language. I'll study (favorite language).
I want to order a pizza. I'll order (favorite pizza).
I want to take a trip. I'll fly (favorite airlines).
I want to watch TV tonight. I'll watch (favorite program).
I want to play a record. I'll play (favorite record).
I want to visit a museum. I'll visit (favorite museum).
I want to make some sauce. I'll make (favorite kind of sauce).

D. Questions to ask the students. Have them ask each other these questions:

If you buy a car, what kind will you buy?
If you order wine, what kind will you order?
If you see a movie, what movie will you see?
If you drink a beer, what beer will you have?
If you have a dessert, what dessert will you have?
If you eat ice cream, what flavor will you have?
If you buy perfume, what brand will you buy?
If you buy a candy bar, what kind will you buy?
If you buy cigarettes, what brand will you buy?
If you go to the university, what will you study?
If you study tonight, what won't you do?
If you take a trip, where won't you go?
If you have a toothache, what won't you eat?
If you have a test, what won't you do?
If you don't have money, what won't you do?
If you don't have homework, what won't you do?

DRILL 96 To contrast *if* and the *first conditional* and *when* and the present tense

T: I might go to (Paris) on my vacation. I want to see (the Eiffel Tower).
S1: *If I go to Paris, I'll see the Eiffel Tower.*
T: I plan to fly to (Paris).
S2: *When I go to Paris, I'll fly (Air France).*

London/Big Ben/BEA
New York/the Empire State Building/TWA
Rome/the Colosseum/Alitalia
India/the Taj Mahal/Air India
Amsterdam/the windmills/KLM
Berlin/the Berlin Wall/Lufthansa
Athens/the Parthenon/Olympic Airways
Madrid/the Prado/Iberian
Istanbul/the Topkapi Museum/Turkish Airways
Cairo/the pyramids/Egypt Air

DRILL 97 To practice *unless* in place of *is not* with the *first conditional*

T: If he doesn't study, he'll fail.
S: *Unless he studies, he'll fail.*

If she doesn't eat, she'll get sick.
If he doesn't tell the truth, he'll go to jail.
If he doesn't do his homework, he'll get a low grade.
If he doesn't practice, he won't make the team.
If he doesn't call Mary, she won't talk to him.
If he doesn't go into the Army, he'll go to jail.
If he doesn't write her, he won't get a letter.
If he doesn't take a taxi, he'll be late.
If he doesn't go to bed early, he'll be tired.
If he doesn't take an umbrella, he'll get wet.
If he doesn't make a reservation, he won't get a room.
If he doesn't set the alarm, he won't get up.
If he doesn't go on the trip, he'll be disappointed.
If he doesn't come soon, Mary will be angry.

The Second Conditional: present unreal
Used when the condition is *not possible* or *unreal* and the result refers to a
present or *future* situation
    condition—past tense
    result—would/could + verb stem

DRILL 98   To practice the *second conditional* with *unreal* possibilities

A.   T: Judy is overweight. You are not Judy.   (go on a diet)
        S: *If I were overweight like Judy, I would go on a diet right now!*

Judy is tired. You are not Judy.   (take a rest)
Judy is bored. You are not Judy.   (read a good book)
Judy is lonely. You are not Judy.   (visit a friend)
Judy is afraid. You are not Judy.   (stay with a friend)
Judy is sick. You are not Judy.   (see a doctor)
Judy is exhausted. You are not Judy.   (go to bed)
Judy is confused. You are not Judy.   (see the teacher)
Judy is hungry. You are not Judy.   (eat a sandwich)
Judy is thirsty. You are not Judy.   (have a glass of water)
Judy is cold. You are not Judy.   (put on a sweater)
Judy is hot. You are not Judy.   (take off my sweater)
Judy is dirty. You are not Judy.   (take a bath)

B.   T: Bob has a car.   (drive to school)
        S: *If I had a car, I would drive to school.*

Bob has a million dollars.   (travel around the world)
Bob has a new house.   (buy a lot of furniture)
Bob has a boat.   (go fishing every day)

Bob has a tennis racket.   (take tennis lessons)
Bob has a bad cold.   (take some medicine)
Bob has a new coat.   (wear it every day)
Bob has a color TV.   (watch TV all day)
Bob has a new motorcycle.   (take you for a ride)
Bob has a new dog.   (walk it in the park)
Bob has a new bicycle.   (ride it every day)
Bob has a new stereo.   (play all my records)

C. T: What would you do if you (were sick)?
    S1: *If I were sick, I would see a doctor.*
    T: What wouldn't you do if you were sick?
    S2: *If I were sick, I wouldn't go to work.*

had a lot of money	had a vacation next week
were President	lost all your money
had a test today	were 10 feet tall
were in London now	worked 16 hours a day
had a motorcycle	taught this class
were 5 years old	were invisible

D. T: Use the following list of animals as "cues" or write the names on slips of paper and give to the students to ask the class.
    (cat)   If I were this animal, I would (catch mice).
    S: (guessing) *If you were a cat, you would catch mice.*

dog	frog
monkey	turtle
elephant	chicken
horse	pig
lion	snake
camel	giraffe
bird	anteater
fish	beaver
duck	

E. T: What language would you speak if you were a(n) Frenchman?
    S: *If I were a Frenchman, I would speak French.*

Greek	Kenyan
Turk	Filipino
Egyptian	Syrian
Spaniard	South African
Brazilian	Nigerian
German	American
Japanese	Pole
Russian	Dutchman
Dane	

DRILL 99   To practice the *second conditional* to give advice

T: Jim wants to buy a used car.
     The car is in bad condition.
S: *If I were Jim, I wouldn't buy that car.*

John wants to borrow $50 from Jim.
John already owes Jim $100.

Bob is overweight.
He wants to eat a big piece of cake.

Judy wants to smoke another cigarette.
She has just put one out.

Jack wants to go outside.
It's cold and he doesn't want to wear a coat.

Mary has a headache.
She doesn't want to take an aspirin.

Judy wants to wear her new white shoes.
The streets are muddy.

John wants to change jobs.
The new job pays less money.

Betty never looks attractive.
She doesn't wear lipstick.

Jane can't save money.
She spends all of her money.

John has a test tomorrow.
He plans to watch TV.

Jim wants to stay at the new hotel.
The food there is terrible.

The Third Conditional: past unreal
Used when the condition in the past was *not possible* or *unreal* and the result
refers to a *past* situation
     condition—past perfect tense
     result—would/could—have + verb stem

DRILL 100   To practice the *third conditional* with *unreal* possibilities in the
past

A.   T: Why didn't you (go to the party)?   (have an invitation)
     S: *I would have gone to the party if I had had an invitation.*

order a steak   (be hungry)
buy the house   (have the money)
telephone Judy   (have her number)
go to Canada   (have time off from work)
write Jane a letter   (have her address)
wear your raincoat   (not take it to the cleaners)
use your pen   (not lose it)
pass the test   (study for it)
become a doctor   (pass the exam)
wash the clothes   (have some soap)
drive the car   (not run out of gas)
take a nap   (not be tired)
go to the football game   (have a ticket)
stay for the lecture   (not be so bored)
buy that dress   (have the money)

B.   T: What would you have been if you had been   (Chopin)
           (a famous composer)
     S: *If I had been Chopin, I would have been a famous composer.*

Napoleon   (a famous emperor)
Eisenhower   (a famous general)
Babe Ruth   (a famous baseball player)
Marilyn Monroe   (a famous movie star)
Cleopatra   (a famous queen)
Charles de Gaulle   (a famous French leader)
Queen Victoria   (a famous British queen)
Michelangelo   (a famous sculptor)
Marco Polo   (a famous explorer)
Homer   (a famous poet)
Clark Gable   (a famous movie star)
Mozart   (a famous composer)
Rembrandt   (a famous painter)
Alexander Graham Bell   (a famous inventor)
Madame Curie   (a famous scientist)
Shakespeare   (a famous playwright)

C.   T: What would you have done if you had been (Michelangelo)?
           (paint the Sistine Chapel)
     S: *If I had been Michelangelo, I would have painted the Sistene Chapel.*

Karl Marx   (write *Das Kapital*)
Columbus   (discover America)
Babe Ruth   (play baseball)
Marco Polo   (travel to China)

Alexander Graham Bell   (invent the telephone)
Magellan   (sail around the world)
Charles Dickens   (write *David Copperfield*)
Cortez   (conquer Mexico)
Madame Curie   (discover radium)
Leonardo da Vinci   (paint the Mona Lisa)
John Lennon   (write a lot of songs)
Lindbergh   (fly solo over the Atlantic)
Admiral Byrd   (discover the South Pole)
Shakespeare   (write *Hamlet*)
Davy Crockett   (die at the Alamo)
Beethoven   (write 9 symphonies)
Noah   (build an ark)

Note: *Students can make up their own "clues" and ask the other students to guess who the famous person is.*

S1:   *If I had been this person, I would have written Macbeth.*

S2:   (guessing) *If you had been Shakespeare, you would have written Macbeth!*

D.   T: What language would you have learned if you had been born in (Italy)?

S: *If I had been born in Italy, I would have learned Italian.*

France	Syria
Greece	South Africa
Turkey	Holland
Egypt	Canada
Spain	the Philippines
Brazil	Thailand
Japan	Burma
Germany	Vietnam
Russia	Mexico
Denmark	Sweden
Kenya	Switzerland

E.   T: What religion would you have practiced if you had been born in (Italy)?

S: *If I had been born in Italy, I would have practiced Catholicism.*

Israel	Greece
Japan	China
India	Germany
Syria	Utah
England	Pennsylvania
Thailand	Texas

DRILL 101   To practice the *first, second,* and *third conditionals*

A.   T: If I had the time . . .   (read a book a day)
      S: *If I had the time, I would read a book a day.*

Wouldn't you be frightened if . . .   (see a lion)
If I had been in your place . . .   (be angry)
If it rains . . .   (call off the picnic)
John wouldn't have a cold . . .   (wear a raincoat)
If you had taken a taxi . . .   (be here earlier)
Wouldn't you be happy if . . .   (have a million dollars)
If you were tired . . .   (go to bed)
Wouldn't you have seen the museum . . .   (have the time)
If I get sick . . .   (see the doctor)
If there had been an accident . . .   (see it on the news)
Wouldn't John call . . .   (be sick)
If I had been born in Italy . . .   (learn Italian)
If Bill had asked her . . .   (not go with John)
I would go to the beach . . .   (not have school)
If you had asked me . . .   (tell you)
If I have the money . . .   (buy a car)
Won't you come . . .   (have the chance)
I would visit Mary . . .   (have the time)
Wouldn't you have called him . . .   (find the number)

B.   T: If I go to London, I will see Big Ben.
            (You're not going to London.)
      S1:   *If I went to London, I would see Big Ben.*
      T: (You didn't go to London.)
      S2:   *If I had gone to London, I would have seen Big Ben.*

If Judy sees John, she will tell him.
(You're not seeing John.)
(You didn't see John.)

If Bob gets the job, he will move to Chicago.
(You're not getting the job.)
(You didn't get the job.)

If Judy calls, Bob will give her the message.
(You're not talking to her.)
(You didn't talk to her.)

If the dress fits, Betty will buy it.
(The dress doesn't fit you.)
(Betty bought the dress.)

If the room is dirty, Mary will clean it.
(Your room is clean.)
(Your room was cleaned last week.)

If John is tired, he will go to bed.
(You're not tired.)
(You weren't tired last night.)

If Jack gets the tickets, he will go to the game.
(You don't have tickets.)
(You didn't have tickets for last week's game.)

If Jack's hungry, he will eat a sandwich.
(You're not hungry.)
(You weren't hungry last night.)

If Mark buys a TV, he will watch the new program.
(You don't have a TV.)
(You didn't have a TV last night.)

If Mary goes to Paris, she will see the Eiffel Tower.
(You're not going to Paris.)
(You didn't go to Paris.)

Wishes and Hopes

		Wishes (at the Moment of Speaking)
Wishes about the future		*Future unreal situation* (would + V-stem)
	I wish	John would study. (He won't.)
Wishes about the present		*Present unreal situation* (were + V-ing)
	I wish	John were studying now. (He's not studying now.) (V-ed)
	I wish	John studied every day. (He doesn't.)
Wishes about the past		*Past unreal situation* (had + V-ed, en)
	I wish	John had studied last night. (He didn't.)

		Wishes (Expressed Before the Moment of Speaking)
At that time in the past		*Unreal situation true at that past moment* (V-ed)
	Last night, I wished	I had a new dress.
About past actions		*Unreal past situation that occurred before that moment* (had + V-ed, en)
	Last night, I wished	I had bought a new dress.

		Hopes (at the Moment of Speaking)
Hopes about the future		*Future real possibility* (will + V-stem) or (*be* going to + V-stem)
	I hope	John will come early. John is going to come early.
Hopes about the past		*Past real possibility* (V-ed)
	I hope	John saw the movie last night. (have + V-ed, en)
	I hope	John has seen the movie by now.

Wish

Used to express a desire that is not likely to be fulfilled or refers to an unreal possibility

DRILL 102   To practice *wishes* about future events or situations (present wishing/future situations)

A.   T: John will be late.
        S: *I wish John wouldn't be late.*

        T: John won't come.
        S: *I wish John would come.*

Betty will pay for lunch.
Bob won't fix the radio.
Tom won't clean his room.
Judy will cook lunch.
The car won't start.
Mary won't take care of her plants.
Bob won't meet us later.
Bob will play cards tonight.
The TV won't work.
Susan will spend all her money.
Michael won't wash his clothes.
This pen won't write.
Janet won't wash her hair.
John will play football this afternoon.
George won't cook.
Steven will buy the tickets.
The iron won't heat up.

B.   T: Judy will gain weight if she eats that cake.
        S: *I wish Judy wouldn't eat that cake.*

Bob will get tired if he runs in that race.
Michael will fail the test if he doesn't study.
Judy will get a cold if she doesn't wear a sweater.
Bob will be late if he doesn't get up soon.
Mary will spend all her money if she buys that coat.
Steven will get the flu if he doesn't see a doctor.
John will lose a lot of money if he bets on that horse.
Robert will get a headache if he doesn't wear glasses.

John will lose his friends if he keeps complaining all the time.
Mary will pay a fine if she doesn't return those library books.
Cathy will be angry if Bob doesn't call her.

DRILL 103   To practice *wishes* about present events or situations (present wishing/present situation)

A.   T: It's raining today.
     S: *I wish it weren't raining.*
     T: The coffee isn't hot.
     S: *I wish the coffee were hot.*

The coat is expensive.	The test is difficult.
I'm sick.	John is late.
The train is late.	Dinner isn't ready.
The flight is canceled.	The house is old.
The beer isn't cold.	School isn't closed.
The baby is crying.	John isn't coming.
The food is cold.	The milk is spoiled.
John isn't happy.	The children aren't here.
The phone is ringing.	Coffee is expensive.
My mother is calling me.	Mary isn't ready.
Bob isn't buying a car.	

B.   T: John visits me every day.
     S: *I wish John didn't visit me every day.*

The mail doesn't come every day.	The movie starts early.
The teacher gives a quiz every day.	Jack smokes a lot.
I have to do my homework.	The windows don't close.
I eat a lot of candy.	The radio doesn't work.
John drinks beer every night.	The clock doesn't tick.
The TV doesn't work.	The students don't study.

C.   T: I can't play tennis.
     S: *I wish I could play tennis.*

Judy can't ski.	Jack can't sleep with the light on.
John can't go.	John can't visit me.
Mary can't cook.	Bill can't help me.
Bill can't find the car keys.	Bob can't sing.
I can't type.	Susan can't come over tonight.
Bob can't speak French.	Bill can't dance.
I can't find Betty.	

D.   T: I don't have a lot of money.
     S: *I wish I had a lot of money.*

The store is closed.	The children can't fall asleep.
School starts early.	I don't have a driver's license.
Bob doesn't do his homework.	I'm doing my homework.
The room is hot.	The water is cold.
The teacher is sick.	The lecture is long.
I can't swim.	The iron doesn't work.
John is taking a trip.	The sky is cloudy.
The walls need painting.	I can't dance.
The car doesn't start.	The stereo is broken.
The dog is barking.	

E.   T: If I had the money, I would go to Europe.
     S: *I wish I had the money to go to Europe.*

If I had the time, I would go shopping.
If I had the money, I would buy a house.
If I had a stamp, I would mail this letter.
If I had a piano, I would practice every day.
If I had a racket, I would play tennis every afternoon.
If I had a stereo, I would play all my records.
If I had a wok, I would make Chinese food.
If I had $20,000, I would buy a Mercedes.
If I had tickets, I would go to the football game.
If I had a horse, I would take it for a ride.
If I had a boat, I would go fishing every day.

DRILL 104   To practice *wishes* about past events or situations (present wishing/past situations)

A.   T: I didn't study for the test yesterday.
     S: (now) *I wish I had studied for the test.*

John didn't invite me to the party.
I didn't pay the telephone bill.
Betty didn't call me yesterday.
I didn't see the play.
I didn't buy the right size shoes.
I didn't take English lessons.
John didn't take me to the movies.
I didn't find the money.
Betty didn't bring the book.
I didn't take the earlier flight.

I didn't give Jack a birthday present.
John didn't send me a postcard.

B.   T: (Yesterday), I got home at 7 o'clock.   (late)
       S: *I wish I hadn't been late.*

I worked all day.   (tired)
I had a fight with John.   (angry)
I had a high fever.   (sick)
I was very nervous.   (upset)
I cleaned the house from top to bottom.   (exhausted)
I didn't say hello to anyone.   (rude)
I didn't have time for lunch.   (busy)
I didn't want to see anyone.   (depressed)
I sat around the house all day.   (bored)
I slept until 12 noon.   (lazy)

C.   T: I couldn't go to the party.
       S: *I wish I could have gone to the party.*

       T: I wouldn't ask him for help.
       S: *I wish I would have asked him for help.*

I couldn't take his picture.
John couldn't take me to the dance.
I wouldn't have time to see the museum.
The teacher wouldn't postpone the test.
John couldn't get the car.
Mary wouldn't listen to me.
I couldn't remember his telephone number.
John wouldn't cancel his trip.
The stereo wouldn't work.
Mary couldn't take the trip.
Bob wouldn't help us.
Susan couldn't get into the university.

D.   T: If I had studied for the test yesterday, I would have passed.
       S: *I wish I had studied for the test yesterday.*

If I had gone on a diet last month, I would have lost 20 pounds (by
    now).
If I had been born in Italy, I would have learned Italian.
If I had bought the tickets, I would have gone to the game today.
If I had read the newspaper, I would have known about the bank
    robbery.
If I had remembered your telephone number, I would have called you
    last night.
If I had had the time, I would have visited you.

If I had bought the record, I would have played it.
If I had known the answer, I would have told you.
If I had planted a garden, I would have had fresh vegetables last summer.
If I had read the book, I would have known the plot of the movie.
If I had gotten an invitation, I would have taken you to the party.

E. T: John went to bed late. Now, he's tired.
    S: *He wishes he had gone to bed early last night.*

John didn't pay the gas bill last week. The gas is off now.
John couldn't go to Mary's party last night. She isn't talking to him today.
Mary got angry last night. She's upset today.
John didn't water his plants. Now they're dead.
John drank 6 beers last night. He has a headache today.
Mary ate a snack every night last week. She's gained 10 pounds.
John didn't put air in his tires. He has 2 flat tires now.
Mary couldn't go to the library yesterday. Now her books are overdue.
John was sick last week. He has a lot of homework to do.
Mary didn't see the new movie. It's not playing in the city any more.
John forgot to send his mother a birthday card. Now she's angry with him.
Mary didn't wear a hat yesterday. Now she has a cold.

DRILL 105   To practice *present wishing* with present and past situations

T: John can't come.
S: *He wishes he could come.*
T: John couldn't come ysterday.
S: *He wishes he could have come yesterday.*

Mary works every night.
Mary worked every night last week.

Betty forgets her book every day.
Betty forgot her book yesterday.

George won't talk to me.
George wouldn't talk to me last night.

Jack is late every day.
Jack was late yesterday.

Betty doesn't know how to bake cookies.
Betty didn't know how to bake the special Christmas cookies.

Bob doesn't write letters.
Bob didn't write me a letter.

The store is closed on Sundays.
The store was closed yesterday.

John doesn't study English.
John didn't study English in school.

Betty won't listen to me.
Betty wouldn't listen to me.

John practices football every day.
John practiced football all afternoon.

Judy is upset.
Judy was upset last night.

The car won't work.
The car wouldn't work yesterday.

John can't come to dinner.
John couldn't come to dinner last week.

DRILL 106 To practice past wishes with past situations (past wishing/past situations)

A.   T: (have a teddy bear)
      S: *When I was a child, I wished I had a teddy bear.*

have a red bicycle	have a pony
can go swimming every day	be a cowboy
can play all day	have a swing in the backyard
can play with my father all the time	be a soldier
can stay up late	can watch TV all day

Note: *Ask the students what they wished they had or did when they were children:*

      When I was a child, I wished I had a _____ .
      When I was a child, I wished I V + ed.

B.   T: Judy is telling her friend about the party she went to last night.
      S: *I had three plates of food!*   *(eat a lot)*
      S: *When I got home, I wished I hadn't eaten a lot.*

I had ten martinis!   (drink so much)
I had a fight with John!   (get angry at my boyfriend)
I dropped a drink!   (spill the wine)
I tore my gown!   (ruin my dress)
I tripped over a chair!   (fall down)
I felt dizzy and had a stomachache!   (get sick)
I stayed until 4 a.m.!   (leave late)
I got into an accident on the way back!   (crash the car)
I regretted going to the party!   (go to the party)

Hope

Used to express a desire that is expected to be fulfilled or, at least, is a real possibility

DRILL 107   To practice *hopes* about *present or future real* possibilities

T: John is in town.   (visit me)
S1: *I hope he will visit me.*
S2: *I hope he's going to visit me.*
S3: *I hope he can visit me.*

Betty is baking a cake.   (give me a piece)
Bob is traveling to Europe.   (go to Paris)
Jim is driving to school.   (pick me up)
Susan is studying for the test.   (help me)
The repairman is looking at the TV.   (fix it)
John is buying the ice cream.   (get chocolate)
Dan is coming from Boston.   (arrive for dinner)
Janet is taking the test for the university.   (pass it)
John is buying the tickets.   (get good seats)
Bob is coming over.   (bring some pizza)
Bill is betting on a horse.   (make some money)
Mary is singing in the talent show.   (win first prize)

DRILL 108   To practice *hopes* about *past real* possibilities

T: John left late for work this morning.   (get there on time)
S: *I hope he got there on time.*
T: They were waiting for John when I left.   (arrive by now)
S: *I hope he has arrived by now.*
T: She has been waiting in line for 3 hours.   (get tickets by now)
S: *I hope she has gotten tickets by now.*

Betty baked a cake this afternoon.   (not eat by now)
Jim took the exam today.   (get a good grade)
Barbara was making a dress this afternoon.   (finish by now)
Robert bought a new car.   (not spend all his money)
Jack went on a diet last month.   (lose weight)
Susan went for a walk in the rain.   (take an umbrella)
Linda has been traveling in Spain.   (enjoy herself)

David received a letter from Mary.   (send her a reply)

Janet was writing the report when I left.   (finish it)

John was coughing all night.   (see the doctor)

Bill took a book out from the library 6 weeks ago.   (return it by now)

Jack took a vacation.   (get some rest)

Mary got a parking ticket last month.   (pay the fine)

John asked the boss for a raise this morning.   (get the raise)

Wishes and Hopes

DRILL 109   To contrast *present hoping* with *present wishing*

T: John's mother lives in the next town.   (visit her)

S: *He hopes she can visit him.*

T: John's mother lives in Australia.

S: *He wishes she could visit him.*

Jim has a job interview tomorrow.   (get a job)

Jim can't find a job.

Judy invited John to the party next Saturday.   (come)

Judy invited John to the party, but he's leaving town tomorrow.

Jack puts money in the bank every week.   (save money)

Jack spends all his money.

Bob is going on a diet.   (lose weight)

Bob eats five times a day and is always hungry.

Judy has cut down her smoking to 3 cigarettes a day.   (stop smoking)

Judy smokes 2 packs of cigarettes a day.

John's knee is a little sore.   (go skiing)

John's leg is broken.

Janet wears a size 9 dress. This dress is size 9.   (fit her)

Janet wears a size 9 dress. This dress is size 5.

John wants to go fishing. He has time off next week.   (go fishing)

John wants to go fishing. He has a lot of work to do.

Susan knows all the answers on the test.   (get a good grade)

Susan doesn't know the answers for the test.

Bill wants to marry Mary. She loves him.   (marry her)

Bill wants to marry Mary. She loves John.

Modals

To express	Present	Past
Assumptions	Must + V-stem	Must have + V-ed, en
	John *must be* out. (He doesn't answer his phone.) John *must have worked* late. (He's not home yet.)	
Possibility/ conjecture	Might + V-stem	Might have + V-ed, en
	John *might be* sick. (He's not in school.) John *might have missed* the bus. (He's not on the bus.)	
Advisability	Should ⎱ + V-stem Ought to ⎰	Should ⎱ have + V-ed, en Ought to ⎰
	John *should* (ought to) *study*. (The test is Friday.) John *should* (ought to) *have studied*. (He failed the test.)	
Necessity	Has to + V-stem Must	Had to + V-stem - - - -
	John *has to* (must) *study* every day. John *had to study* every day last week.	
Opportunity	Could + V-stem	Could have + V-ed, en
	John *could go* to the party. (He has an invitation.) John *could have gone* to the party. (He had an invitation; he didn't go.)	
Preference	Would rather + V-stem	Would rather have + V-ed, en
	I *would rather see* the French movie (than the Italian movie). I *would rather have seen* the French movie (than the Italian movie) last night.	
Ability	Can ⎱ + V-stem Am able to ⎰	Could ⎱ + V-stem Was able to ⎰
	I *can* (am able to) *play* tennis. I *could* (was able to) *play* tennis when I was in high school.	
Past habits	Used to/would + V-stem	
	I *used to play* tennis every day. (I don't any more.) I *would play* tennis every day. (I don't any more.)	
Suggestions	Let's/should/had better + V-stem	
	Let's take the bus. We *should take* the train. We *had better take* a taxi.	
Permission	May/could/can + V-stem	
	May I *go* now? (especially polite) *Could* I *go* now? (polite) *Can* I *go* now? (informal)	
Polite requests	Would like + N / Would like to + V	
	Would you *like* some coffee? *Would* you *like to have* some coffee?	

Used as auxiliaries to the main verb to indicate meanings, such as probabilities, recommendations, and approvals, that the speaker wants to express

Note: *The modals are difficult for students whose native languages do not make these distinctions in this way.*

DRILL 110   To contrast *must* (assumption) and *might* (possibility) with present sitautions

Note: Must be *is used when the speaker is* almost *convinced that an event is true.* (Will be *is used if he is* totally *convinced.)* Might be *is used to express less probability that an event is true.*

T: John's not in class today.   (be absent)
S: *John must be absent from school.*
T: John's late for school today.
S: *John might be absent.*

Jim is shivering.   (be cold)
Jim is wearing a sweater.
Judy is opening the mailbox.   (send a letter)
Judy is buying stamps.
Betty is sitting at the desk, looking at her English book and writing.
   (do homework)
Betty is sitting at the desk.
John is signing his paycheck at the teller's window.   (cash a check)
John is at the bank.
John is holding his mouth and entering the dentist's office.   (have
   a toothache)
John is holding his mouth.
John is carrying a bag of garbage.   (put out the garbage)
John is carrying a bag.
There is someone at the door with a rack of milk.   (be the milkman)
There is someone at the door.
John ate 4 cherry pies and his face is green; he can barely stand up.
   (be sick)
John ate 4 cherry pies.

DRILL 111   To contrast *should* (suggestion) and *must/have to* (necessity) with present situations

Note: Must/have to *is used by the speaker when the* advice *is considered very necessary;* should *is used with less important recommendations.*

T: Mary has a cold.   (see a doctor)
S: *Mary should see a doctor.*
T: Mary broke her leg.
S: *Mary must see a doctor!*
or *Mary has to see a doctor.*

Mary barely passed the test.   (study)
Betty has failed every test.

The library books are due next week.   (Judy/return the books)
The library books are due today.

The car is making a funny noise.   (John/take it to the mechanic)
The car broke down.

I'm going to France.   (get a vaccination)
I'm going to France.   (get a passport)

The telephone bill is due next week.   (John/pay the bill)
The telephone bill is due today.

I'm flying to Florida sometime in the summer.   (make a reservation)
I'm flying to Florida on a holiday weekend.

John wants to be a businessman.   (go to college)
John wants to be a doctor.

My father is overweight.   (go on a diet)
My father is 50 pounds overweight, has a heart condition, and is 70
  years old.

DRILL 112   To contrast the use of *may, can,* and *could* to express permission

  may—very formal; used when speaking to older people or important
people whenever a "polite" form is indicated
  can—used informally with friends, children, or peers
  could—acceptable to everyone

T: (to a priest)   (help)
S: *May I help you?*

T: (to your little sister)   (clean your room)
S: *Can you clean your room now?*

T: (to a bank teller)   (cash this check)
S: *Could you cash this check?*

to a small child   (pick up the toys)
to a shop clerk   (show me a shirt)
to a college professor   (take your course)
to your best friend   (meet me later)

to your secretary   (type this report)
to your little brother   (play outside)
to a policeman   (give me directions)
to a telephone operator   (get me a Boston number)
to a judge   (leave the court)
to your roommate   (wake me up early)

DRILL 113   To contrast *could* (opportunity) and *should* (advisability) with present situations

T: John was accepted at Harvard and Yale. Harvard gave him a scholarship.
S: *He could go to Harvard or Yale, but he should go to Harvard.*

Mary has free plane tickets to Boston and New York. Her friends are in Boston.
Jim has a steak and a chicken in the fridge. He doesn't like chicken.
Barbara has a bottle of orange juice and a bottle of coke. She has a bad cold.
Mary tried on a fur coat and a cloth coat. She wants to save money.
Jack wants to give Bill the red sweater or the blue one. He likes to wear the blue sweater.
Larry is thinking of buying an automatic-shift or a standard-shift car. The standard-shift car uses less gasoline.
Bob has tickets for a high school football game and for a professional football game.
George wants to take the plane or the train to New York. He doesn't have much time to spend there.
Jack is looking at the hardbound book and the same book in paperback. He doesn't like to waste money.
Betty has a red dress and a green dress. The red dress fits her better.

DRILL 114   To practice the use of *should, had better,* and *let's* to express suggestions

T: (train)   (take)
S1:   *Should we take the train?*
T: (plane)
S2:   *Let's take the plane!*
T: (bus)
S3:   *We had better take the bus.*

milk	(drink)	the red one	(buy)
coke		the blue one	
juice		the green one	

the Chevy	(drive)	the Italian movie	(see)
the Ford		the French movie	
the Volkswagen		the Japanese movie	
the elephants	(feed)	the steak	(order)
the monkeys		the fish	
the lions		the chicken	
the art museum	(visit)	history	(study)
the science museum		math	
the history museum		English	

DRILL 115 To contrast *ought to/should* (suggestion) and *would rather* (preference) with present situations

T: (send Mary a card)
S1: *You ought to send Mary a card.*
or *You should send Mary a card.*
T: (visit her)
S2: *I would rather visit her.*
or *I'd rather visit her.*

do your homework	wear a suit
watch TV	wear blue jeans
clean your room	ask Judy to the party
listen to records	take Betty
wash your hair	write him a letter
wear a wig	telephone him
practice piano	type the report
play tennis	write it by hand
take an umbrella	see the new French movie
wear a raincoat	go to a western
take a bath	read a good book
take a shower	look at a movie magazine

DRILL 116 To contrast *must have* (assumption) and *might have* (conjecture) when speaking in the present, but referring to a situation that occurred in the past

Note: *The past of* must/have to *(necessity) is* had to; must have *does* not *refer to necessity.*

T: John bought a house.   (spend a lot of money)
S: *John must have spent a lot of money.*
T: (buy a duplex)
S: *John might have bought a duplex.*

John got off a plane from Chicago.   (take a trip)
(take a business trip)

Mary had a stomachache.   (feel ill)
(eat spoiled food)

The train is late.   (start off schedule)
(have engine trouble)

George fell down the stairs.   (hurt himself)
(break his leg)

Jack met Judy for lunch.   (talk to each other)
(order the same lunch)

Bob ran in the race yesterday.   (be tired)
(win)

Betty worked until 9 o'clock last night.   (come home late)
(do overtime)

DRILL 117   To practice *should have/ought to have* to express unfulfilled obligation

T: Mary failed the test.   (study last night)
S: *She should have studied last night but she didn't.*
or *She ought to have studied last night but she didn't.*

Betty watched the late movie last night. Now she's tired.   (go to bed earlier)

John forgot to set the alarm clock. He overslept.   (set it)

I ran out of coffee last night.   (buy some last week)

The ice cream melted overnight.   (eat it last night)

The fire burned out.   (put on more logs)

The cake burned in the oven.   (take it out sooner)

All the shirts are sold out.   (buy one yesterday)

The electric company turned off the electricity.   (pay the bill)

The meat was spoiled.   (not eat it)

The house was a mess when the guests arrived.   (clean)

I can't get a hold of Jim.   (call him yesterday)

John saw the accident but left immediately.   (report it to the police)

My fur coat was stolen at the theater last night.   (not wear it)

I didn't sleep last night.   (drink 4 cups of coffee)

DRILL 118 To practice *could have* (missed opportunity) and *had to* (necessity) when speaking in the present, but referring to a situation that occurred in the past

T: Mary had tickets to the play, but she took care of her little brother instead.

S: *Mary could have gone to the play, but she had to take care of her little brother.*

John had an invitation to dinner, but he did his homework instead.
Betty had a good book to read, but she wrote a composition instead.
Jack had tickets to the football game, but he worked on his car instead.
Bob had a chance to go to Paris, but he worked instead.
Mary had time to take a nap, but she cleaned the house instead.
Bill had a reservation at the French restaurant, but he finished the report instead.
Susan had time to watch TV, but she washed her hair instead.
Tom had a chance to play tennis, but he went to the library instead.

DRILL 119 To practice *would* and *used to* with habits and actions repeated in the past

A.   T: When I was a child, I would   (play every day).
        S1: *I used to play every day.*
        S2: *Did you use to play so often?*
        S3: *Yes, I would play every day.*

read stories with my mother
eat cookies and milk every afternoon
ride my bicycle to school
read comic books in my room
play football with my father
tease my little brother
build model airplanes
play with my puppy

B.   T: When I was single, I used to   (eat out every day).
        S1: *I would eat out every day.*
        S2: *Would you eat out so often?*
        S3: *Yes, I used to eat out every day.*

see all the new movies   drink a lot of beer
go on dates   eat frozen dinners
wash my own clothes   iron my own shirts
have a lot of money   play football with my friends
go away every weekend   spend a lot of money
travel a lot

DRILL 120   To practice *would like to* and *would like* with polite requests

T: (coffee)
S1: *Would you like to have some coffee?*
T: (cup)
S2: *Yes, I'd like a cup, please.*

cake	bread
piece	slice
milk	butter
glass	pat
ice cream	sugar
scoop	spoonful
wine	beer
glass	bottle
candy	pie
piece	slice
tea	
cup	

DRILL 121   To practice *can/could* and *be able/was able* to express ability

T: run 10 miles
S1: *When I was younger, I could run 10 miles, but I can't now.*
S2: *When I was younger, I was able to run 10 miles, but I'm not able to now.*

jump over a high fence	swim 10 miles
ski all day	dance all night
read a book a week	drink a lot of beer
type 60 words a minute	eat all I wanted
play football all afternoon	ride a bicycle for miles
hit a baseball 300 feet	lift 200 pounds

DRILL 122   To review modal auxiliaries used in *present* situations

possibility—might/may
suggestion/should/ought to/had better
necessity—must/have to
conclusion—must
ability—can/be able
having opportunity—could
desirability—would like to

preference—would rather
past habit—would/used to

T: Jane won't visit her aunt. It's her responsibility . . .
S: *Jane should visit her aunt.*

George has a pain in his right side. It's necessary to see a doctor . . .
Betty doesn't have time to see you.
John wants to see you very much.
Mary's lights are out, her car is gone, and no one answers the doorbell.
    I conclude . . .
Jack buys cheap shoes. He prefers expensive shoes.
Susan has a test tomrrow. I advise her to study.
Mary has money to spend. She has the opportunity to go shopping.
Greg always smoked 40 cigarettes a day. He gave it up.
I can take a taxi or a bus. I prefer to take a taxi.
John went to bed early. He was studying for 24 hours. I conclude . . .
Bill can take Mary or Judy to the dance. He likes Mary better.
Jack is 50 pounds overweight. The doctor gave him some advice.
My radio is broken. John knows how to fix it.
Jim was invited to a party but is staying home to read a book. He had
    the opportunity to go to the party.
Linda received a gift from her aunt. It's her obligation to send a thank
    you note.
John is traveling to China. The law requires him to get a visa.
The secretary made some typing errors. She has an eraser.
The sky is getting cloudy. There's a chance of rain.
Michael is traveling to Europe. It's advisable to get a smallpox vaccina-
    tion, but it isn't required.

DRILL 123   To review modal auxiliaries used in *past* situations

past possibility—might have/may have
past conclusion—must have
past obligation—should have
past opportunity—could have
past ability—could
past preference—would rather have

T: I didn't see Bob at the theater. It's possible that I missed him.
S: *I might have missed him.*

Jim caught a cold last week, but he went skiing. Now he's sick.
I didn't see Judy at the party after 10 o'clock. I concluded that she left
    early.
George decided not to come over for dinner. He ate at home instead.

It's possible that Linda worked late last night.

I just got a card from Mary, postmarked from Spain.

John ordered chicken instead of steak. He preferred steak, but it was very expensive.

I told John to lock the car door, but he didn't listen to me. The car was stolen.

Mary drank the coke because the milk was sour. She preferred to have milk.

Betty's birthday was yesterday. I didn't send her a card.

It's possible that he didn't hear what I said, but he was standing next to me.

John didn't offer to take us home. He had the time and the car.

Jim ran very fast when he was in school, but he doesn't train any more.

Mr. Smith paid the gas bill late. The gas was turned off.

There are puddles of water in the street and the sky is still black.

It's possible that Jim had an accident.

The test was given in January, April, August, and November. John had the opportunity to take it any time.

Mary studied French in high school. She can't speak French now.

John didn't put the meat in the fridge. Now it's spoiled.

Bob left with $4000 and returned with a brand-new car.

Mary didn't go to the party. It was necessary to stay home and study.

Passives

	Active voice	Passive voice
Present	We *build* houses.	Houses *are built.*
Present continuous	We *are building* houses.	Houses *are being built.*
Future/modals	We *are going to build* houses.	Houses *are going to be built.*
	We *will build* houses.	Houses *will be built.*
	We *must build* houses.	Houses *must be built.*
Past	We *built* houses.	Houses *were built.*
Past continuous	We *were building* houses . . .	Houses *were being built* . . .
Present perfect	We *have built* houses . . .	Houses *have been built* . . .
Past perfect	We *had built* houses . . .	Houses *had been built* . . .
Future perfect	We *will have built* houses . . .	Houses *will have been built* . .

Used when the subject of the verb is the *receiver* of the action of the verb

Note: *Passive construction requires the use of a form of the verb* to be *with the past participle of the action verb.*

DRILL 124   To practice the passive form of the *present simple tense*

T: The state builds new roads every year.
S: *New roads are built every year.* (by the state)

We need action now.	We need food.
They spend $100 every week.	The secretary opens the mail.
The government builds roads.	We speak English here.
That store sells furniture.	Students lose many books.

DRILL 125   To practice the *passive* form of the *present continuous tense*

T: Miss Jones is writing the report.
S: *The report is being written.* (by Miss Jones)

They are sending the message.	The actors are performing the play.
He is delivering the mail.	The man is washing the car.
She is preparing the dinner.	The men are building the house.
The teacher is giving the test.	Someone is using the telephone.

DRILL 126   To practice the *passive* form of the *future tense* and *modal auxiliaries*

A.   T: John is going to fix the radio.
      S: *The radio is going to be fixed.* (by John)

The men are going to build a road.
The children are going to visit the teacher.
They are going to return the book.
She is going to bake cookies.
Jack is going to write letters.
Someone is going to take the students to the museum.
The principal is going to examine the students.
Someone is going to deliver the mail.

B.   T: Jack will write the report tonight.
      S: *The report will be written tonight.* (by Jack)

Jack can fix the radio.
Judy will call Mary tonight.
They might raise the price of coffee.
Bill should send the check.
The secretary will type the letter.
The students will write the compositions.
The children must eat lunch.
The men will build the house.

DRILL 127   To practice *passive* forms of *present* and *future tense* verbs

A.   T: We must stop war.
      S: *War must be stopped.*

We should build more hospitals now.
We are serving the guests.
We write reports every day.
We can fix the chair.
We must build more houses.
We are going to send the children to school.
We study the exercises carefully.
We will deliver the newspapers.
We should send the telegram.
We are going to build roads.
We can repair the car.
We need good leaders in this country.
We will invite them to the party.
We speak English in class.

We must type the letters.
We are cleaning the house.

B.   T: Someone wants to use the telephone.   (use) The phone . . .
           S: *The phone is being used right now.*

Will you finish the report soon?   (finish)
By tonight, the report . . .

The students must write compositions for homework.   (write)
Tonight, the compositions . . .

Has the mail arrived?   (deliver)
Right now, the mail . . .

How long do you have to cook the chicken?   (cook)
The recipe says that the chicken . . .

The government plans to build a new highway.   (build)
In 19 _____, the new highway . . .

Will there be dancing at the wedding?   (play)
From 7 to 9 o'clock, music . . .

The price of sugar is going up.   (raise)
The price of sugar . . .

Are we having coffee on the balcony?   (serve)
Coffee . . .

Where can I buy inexpensive furniture?   (sell)
Cheap furniture . . .

Does anyone speak English at that hotel?   (speak)
English . . .

DRILL 128   To practice the passive form of the *past simple tense*

T: Jack built the house.
S: *The house was built.* (by Jack)

The students wrote the compositions.
Someone delivered the mail.
They served dinner at 8 o'clock.
The secretary typed the letter.
We returned the books.
The children cleaned the room.
We did the work.
The teachers gave the test.

DRILL 129   To practice the passive form of the *past continuous tense*

T: Mary was writing letters.
S: *Letters were being written.* (by Mary)

They were dividing the money.
Someone was delivering the package.
We were answering the phones.
The secretary was typing the report.
She was baking cookies.
The students were writing the exercises.
Someone was building the roads.
We were serving dinner.

DRILL 130   To practice the passive form of the *present perfect tense*

T: We have built the house.
S: *The house has been built.* (by us)

Someone has delivered the mail.
Jack has written the letters.
They have typed the report.
Someone has served the food.
The students have written the exercises.
We have sent the information.
They have invited the guests.
We have returned the book.

DRILL 131   To practice the passive form of the *past perfect tense*

T: Bob had written the report (before he came).
S: *The report had been written* (before he came).

They had made the phone call.
We had prepared lunch.
We had written the letters.
The students had done the exercises.
They had completed the lesson.
We had returned the book.
He had mailed the letter.
They had locked the door.

DRILL 132   To practice the passive form of the *future perfect tense*

T: Bill will have written the report (by Saturday).
S: *The report will have been written* (by Saturday).

We will have washed the car.
They will have finished the house.
They will have bought the furniture.
The students will have taken the test.
We will have done the homework.
The secretary will have typed the report.
We will have sent the letter.
The students will have taken the examination.

DRILL 133   To practice the passive forms of *past tense verbs*

A.   T: We sent the letter.
     S: *The letter was sent* (by us).

We have built the roads.
We will have cleaned the house (by Saturday).
We had cooked dinner (before you came).
We divided the money.
We had typed the letter (before we left).
We will have completed this class (before the summer).
We washed the car.
We were ordering dinner.
We have selected the wine.
We opened the mail.
We will have written the exercises (by Monday).
We turned on the TV.
We were eating lunch.
We have considered the question.
We will have sold the car (by next week).
We locked the door.

B.   T: Had he typed the report when he called?   (type) The report . . .
     S: *The report had been typed when he called.*

Have you cooked dinner yet?   (prepare)
By 7 o'clock, the dinner . . .

Did the professor start the lecture?   (give)
The lecture . . .

Have you applied to the university yet?   (send)
The application . . .

Did Mary invite a lot of people to the party?   (invite)
50 people . . .

Has John fixed the TV yet?   (repair)
The TV ...

Did Bob take his books back to the library?   (return)
The books ...

Did I miss lunch?   (serve)
The sandwiches ...

Had he fed the cat before he left?   (feed)
The cat ...

DRILL 134   To review the *passive* forms of all verbs

T: We are writing the report.
S: *The report is being written.*

We make progress every day.
We should review the lesson.
We painted the walls.
We are preparing lunch.
We will have received the letter (by Saturday).
We have made the salad.
We were playing the radio.
We had cleaned the house (before they came).
We are going to type the letters.
We served coffee.
We were playing cards.
We will have ordered the furniture (by next week).
We are paying bills.
We must solve the problem.
We have ordered the flowers.
We speak correct English in class.
We had eaten dessert (when they came).
We took the test.
We need food.
We will send the package.
We are going to wash the car.
We might paint the house.
We were fixing the car.
We mailed the letters.
We need hospitals.
We should iron the shirts.
We have read the paper.
We typed the report.
We will send the package.
We have considered the question.